ArtEZ Press

DRAPING
> Art and craftsmanship in fashion design

Preface

'Being a fashion designer not only requires having a clear vision, but also being able to communicate that vision to the people who actually make the clothes. Actually, as a designer you spend most of your time trying to solve technical problems. Being able to drape has always been of great help to me in finding solutions to these problems, since it makes one understand how a piece of fabric moves around the body. Through draping the two-dimensional becomes three-dimensional. This book provides insight in the basic principles of draping.'

Lucas Ossendrijver
Head of the design department of Lanvin Homme, Paris

Once you have practiced and mastered this inspiring technique, you can create a new world of shapes and designs.

Annette Duburg and Rixt van der Tol

1 INTRODUCTION AND HISTORY

In dialogue with the cloth:

11 > History
11 > Greeks and
     Romans

11 > Development of
     pattern cutting
13 > Haute couture

15 > Application:
     couture versus
     ready-to-wear

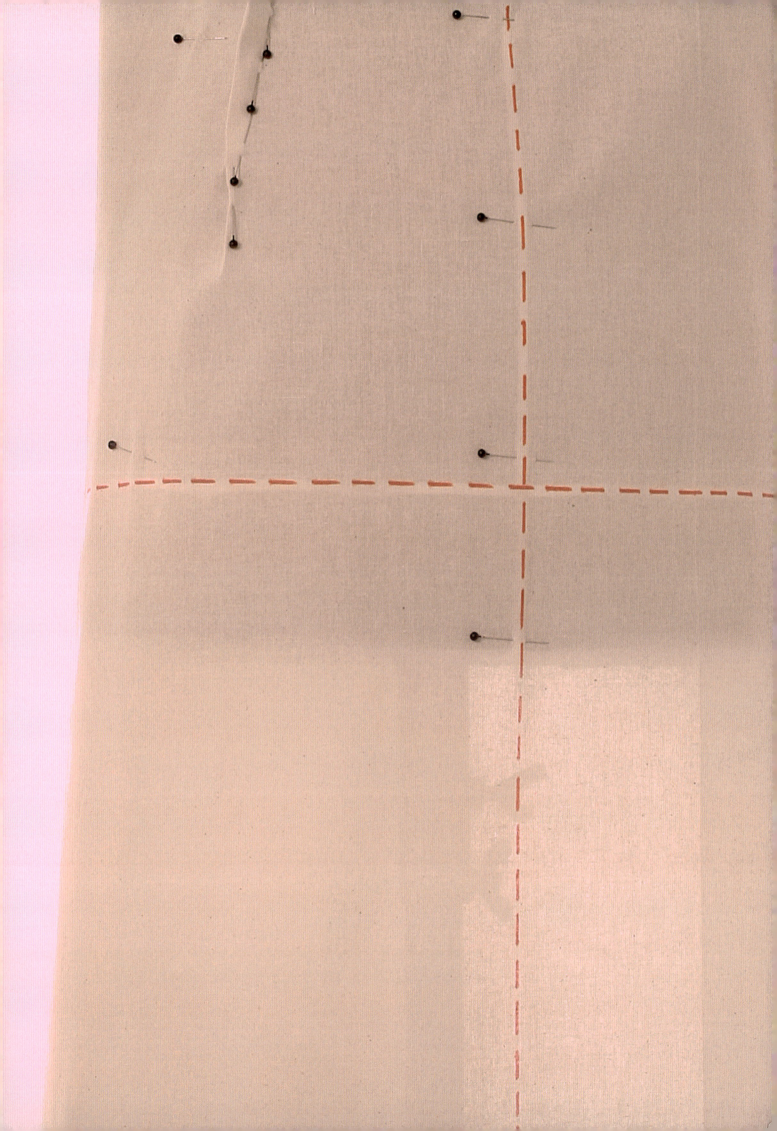

In dialogue with the cloth

'Draping is a gutter of textile, with narrowings and broadenings, sluices and waterfalls, deltas and stagnant tributaries. (...) Draped cloth is pure energy.' Dirk Lauwaert

Throughout the ages innumerable forms of clothing have appeared and disappeared. According to the English historian of costume James Laver, the construction of all this clothing relies on two basic principles: draping or cutting. In the first case the starting point is the cloth - it is arranged around the body and fastened at strategic points. With cutting, on the other hand, the body is at the forefront - the material is cut according to a pattern corresponding to measurements of length and breadth. The separate parts are then sewn together, resulting in a definitive spatial form that can be put on and taken off - in contrast to a draped garment that has no fixed form. These two approaches do not necessarily exclude each other. A combination of draping fabric on the body and making garments to measure is possible by means of the modern art of draping, an exacting craft technique for developing a garment. You could call it sculpting in cloth. It is the soul of haute couture.

>> Until now rather little has been published on the subject of draping. A good understanding of it requires practical experience and a feel for the material. The know-how is traditionally passed on from master to apprentice in the atelier. Nowadays some fashion schools teach draping as a practical part of the course. Some basic theoretical knowledge in support of practice, however, is not an unnecessary luxury. To start with, a definition of the term.

The French term 'moulage' comes from moule, a mould, and originally means forming an object with the aid of a mould. Or, in general, modelling something. Moulage thus means modelling or draping.

>> Draping is a technique that involves working directly in a three-dimensional way. Design and pattern are achieved simultaneously. It is carried out as follows: the cloth (sometimes cut into provisional pattern parts) is arranged in particular forms on a dress stand or a human body. The occasion might be a design sketch or just a rough idea. In so doing, it soon becomes clear where possible corrections are needed and what the cloth itself 'wants'. Sometimes that is something unexpected, something that perhaps generates new ideas that would never exist on paper. A dialogue with the cloth is created, requiring intuition, originality, imagination and craft experience on the part of the designer.

>> This way of working provides great freedom, since draping is not bound to standard sizes and calculations. The only restrictions are the form of the body and the material to be used. It goes without saying that many designers regard draping as an essential part of the design process.

>> Draping should thus lead to the perfecting of a design, as well as to insights concerning its realisation in terms of cutting techniques.

>> The material used for draping is called toile, another French term which simply means fabric. In practice, various qualities of gauze were once used for it. Nowadays unbleached cotton in different thicknesses is used. The important thing is that the cloth is plain and of a neutral light colour so that the picture is not influenced by prints or other processes.

>> The French term for a draped garment is also a toile, and someone who makes toiles is a toiliste or modeliste.

>> As soon as the toile is completed it is taken apart. The separate parts serve as a pattern for the final garment.

>> One advantage of this three-dimensional way of working is that the result is immediately visible, at any moment. With a pattern drawn on paper the final result only reveals itself after it has been executed in cloth.

>> The completed toile does not have to be a draped form per se. Toiles are often in fact architectonically simple but very ingenious forms.

>> Claude Montana once said, 'I thought my first toile was barbaric. Such a form in that awful cotton was hideous. But once you're able to read such a form only then do you see how beautiful it is as a means of expressing what it is you actually want, what you intend.'

'Egechtheion', Athens (Acropolis), ionic temple

In dialogue with the cloth:

> *History*

> *Greeks and
Romans*

> *Development of
pattern cutting*

> History

Draping is a typical phenomenon within the history of Western clothing. The elegantly draped robes from antiquity could be regarded as early predecessors. In later centuries tunic-like garments were worn; it was not until the late middle ages that a certain cut made its appearance. Documentation of genuine drapings, however, did not appear until the nineteenth century.
>> What follows is a brief historical sketch:

> Greeks and Romans

Clothing in the highly developed cultures of ancient Greece (± 600 B.C. - ± 100 B.C.) and the Roman Empire (275 B.C. - 330 A.D.) relied on what James Laver calls the Mediterranean basic principle: predominantly rectangular pieces of fabric of different sizes, depending on the usage and the physical measurements of the wearer. The pieces of fabric were draped, folded and wrapped in different ways and according to certain rules. The chiton, for example, was a rectangular piece of clothing stitched up on one side so as to create a spacious tube that was held together on the shoulders by means of brooches. For the sake of freedom of movement, the volume of cloth was kept in place by bands intersecting each other on the upper part of the body. Another outer garment was the peplos, a rectangular basic form that was not closed with a seam. In both cases one or more belts around the waist were used, thus creating a characteristic blouse effect that is found mainly with female silhouettes. Apart from that, there was virtually no difference between men's and women's clothing.
>> Sometimes the himation was worn over the chiton or peplos, a rectangular over-garment wrapped diagonally around the body so that the fabric gained more elasticity and was more comfortable. Thanks to the numerous methods of draping, various forms were achieved with a very limited number of basic forms.
>> Although the basic form continued to be maintained throughout almost the entire period, there were changes in the way it was expressed. Rather rough, often heavily decorated woollen fabric was used in the early archaic period, while in the subsequent classic period finer fabrics were developed and the use of linen was introduced. The most balanced drapings date from this period (the folds being sometimes made more beautiful with the aid of pieces of lead in the hem). The late Hellenistic period was marked by very wide drapings, with an exaggerated dynamics.
>> Ideals of democracy, humanism and personal freedom were cherished in ancient Greece. Clothing, too, was never forced. The pieces of cloth draped around the body were both comfortable and elegant and in a certain sense can be seen as design based on an ideal of freedom. Man was respected for this original qualities and so were fine woven products - one would never think of brutally cutting pieces out of the cloth or processing it in any way.

The Romans took over many aspects from Greek culture, including, to a certain extent, the style of clothing, although the Romans displayed more of a penchant for beauty and luxuriousness. On the other hand, they were also fond of practical clothing where you did not have to think anew every morning about the style of draping.
>> The garment most worn by men and women from all layers of society was the tunica, a simple, shirt-like garment with well fitting shoulder seams that could be worn as an undergarment as well as an outer garment. The outer garment for women, the stola, is actually a second shirt-form. Drapings were more likely to be found with the palla, the over-garment that is similar to the Greek himation.
>> The national attire and hallmark of the free Roman is the toga. Judging from the elliptical basic form, its origin is probably Etruscan. The original Etruscan toga was a felt-like sash and the way that the toga was later wrapped owed something to this, although it had long been made of woven cloth. Unlike the Greek himation, the toga was not arranged diagonally around the body, but always enclosed the body in a straightforward way as a more autonomous envelope.
>> Initially the toga was a relatively simple, everyday garment, but it gradually evolved into gaudy attire for notables that was later, during the empire, made of expensive fabrics with gold embroidery. The toga became more voluminous and the cloth was folded double before being wrapped. Not only did the volume increase considerably, but the wrapping process became more and more complicated and sophisticated. It is still a mystery how this was done exactly and how it is that the toga did not slip downwards, even though movement was evidently not hindered.

> Development of pattern cutting

Draped and wrapped garments are still used today in some non-Western cultures, well-known examples being the Indian sari and the Indonesian sarong. After the decline of the Roman Empire, however, a new age gradually dawned in Western costume history. The first centuries of our era were dominated by migrations; there is no evidence of noticeable developments in the field of clothing during this period of turmoil. The situation stabilised around the 9th century. In the meantime, Christendom had spread across all of Europe. Clothing in the early middle ages was tunic-like and simple, functional and uniform. Starting in the 12th century,

Dress 1935-1936 Madeleine Vionnet

Madeleine Vionnet drapes a design made to scale on her wooden mannequin

attempts were made to emphasise the body by means of closer fitting garments. But people did not yet know how to make them. Tight sleeves, for example, would be cut extra long and then rolled up so that the transverse pleats would ensure the necessary freedom of movement for the joints. A bit later it was discovered how the use of gores could provide skirts with extra width.

>> Cutting in the sense of ingeniously cut sections that are then sewn together to produce a three-dimensionally fixed whole did not arise until the late 14th century. If you consult the literature on the subject you find an endless series of fashion silhouettes and components; there is plenty of information about the use of colour and material, as well as about all sorts of socio-cultural aspects, but the trajectory between the ideas conceived and their realisation is largely vague. The first book about the art of dressmaking appeared in 1580 in Spain: 'Libro de Geometria. Pratica y Traça' by Juan de Alcega. Patterns were depicted in this and subsequent books, but they were meant to show the tailor how the cloth could be cut as advantageously as possible. It is doubtful whether full-sized paper patterns also existed at that time. In the 19th century a good tailor was still expected to work without paper patterns. The customer was measured with strips of paper (the tape measure did not appear until the mid-19th century) and the tailor would use these measurements to draw the pattern directly onto the cloth.

>> Did draping and modelling exist between the 15th and the 19th centuries? A great many styles can be pointed to that suggest this may have been the case: the high-necked bodices and ruffs at the Spanish court in the 16th century, the voluminously pleated men's trousers during the Baroque period, 'Watteau' pleats or the drapes of a manteau à la polonaise in the 18th century, just to mention a few examples. But nowhere is there any mention of antique draping techniques. This is perhaps because no general system yet existed and tailors more or less invented their own method of creating particular volumes. But the most important reason for this shortage of information is probably the fact that tailors at that time possessed no special status. In most cases we no longer know even their names, let alone any technical details.

> Haute couture

The era of the fashion designer celebrated as an artist dawned in 1858 when the English dressmaker Charles Frederick Worth (1825-1895) opened his salon in Paris. He launched a new approach that revolutionised haute couture: rather than let the customers decide how a dress should look, the master himself designed a collection which he then presented on live models. On the basis of these the customers could make their choice. Worth used toiles, but the customers could choose their own fabrics. He was also the first designer to sign his work.

>> Renowned specifically for her draping applications is Madelaine Vionnet (1876-1975) who was one of the most influential couturiers in the 1920s and 30s. Her great admiration for classical antiquity was possibly a source of inspiration for her use of geometric basic forms that adjusted themselves to the body in a simple and elegant way. Another source of inspiration might well have been her original penchant for mathematics. Her family was too poor to pay for her to study, setting aside the fact that such studies were not customary for girls at that time. At the age of twelve Vionnet apprenticed herself to a clothesmaker on the edge of Paris. Thus began a career which would later earn her the nickname 'Euclid of fashion'.

>> Vionnet's clothing designs are of a sophisticated simplicity, while often they do not immediately reveal their construction; it is not until they are taken apart that you see how they are made. Most of them owe their suppleness and beautiful fall to the fact that they are cut diagonal to the grain of the fabric. The development of this technique was one of Vionnet's greatest merits. She would order fabrics 1.8 metres wider than necessary to give her more freedom in her work.

>> Vionnet experimented with draping on a half-scale dummy. Her innovative way of working and her craftsmanship resulted in draping reaching an unprecedented level. Today she is still an example for many fashion designers.

>> During the heyday of haute couture - up to and including the 1950s - fabulous creations were produced, and draping was used in practically all the ateliers of the great masters. Jacques Heim, for example, created a furore in 1931 with a draped bathing suit. Nina Ricci preferred to use draping on a live model and she also cut a lot on the bias, as did Jacques Griffe who had mastered all the finer points of cutting and draping. Jacques Fath draped not only on a model but also often on himself, observed by a few assistants who immediately made drawings of his discoveries.

>> One of Vionnet's kindred spirits was Alix Grès (pseudonym of Germaine Barton, 1903-1993). Like Vionnet, she designed directly from the material and allowed herself to be guided by the way the fabric fell. Grès's designs were often sculptural and inspired by Greek drapings, often executed in jersey, crêpe or muslin-like cloth. She too possessed an extensive professional skill and many of her creations are cut on the bias. Grès cared little about current fashions. Her designs are famous for their timeless elegance and the way in which they flatter the body.

>> The architectonic constructions by Cristóbal Balenciaga reveal the use of ingenious drapings. Many of his designs stand away from the body so that a special space is created between skin and cloth. Balenciaga had his atelier heads model his design sketches, after which he would then perfect the toiles himself. These sessions could last hours, while

In dialogue with the cloth:

> *Application:*
> *couture versus*
> *ready-to-wear*

Madame Grès

Toiles in the atelier of Yves Saint Laurent

Balenciaga worked concentratedly and in silence on the ultimate form. He was a perfectionist and devoted infinite care to finding the perfect sleeve, for example.
>> Starting in the mid-1960s haute couture lost its authority, without, however, disappearing completely. Yves Saint Laurent counts as the most influential couturier in the second half of the 20th century. For him, too, Madeleine Vionnet was a source of inspiration. During the 1990s, many stuffy fashion houses were brought to life again through the deployment of remarkable young designers like John Galliano for Dior and Nicolas Ghesquière for Balenciaga who seem to have mastered the art of draping just as well as any veteran.
>> In the autumn of 2006 the Greek designer Sophia Kokosalaki was appointed as creative director for the house of Vionnet. Inspired by the style of her ancestors in the antique period, Kokosalaki achieved fame through the application of flowing lines and innovative drapings.

> *Application: couture versus ready-to-wear*

Draping is the ultimate way to realise individuality and exclusiveness. Judging by the amount of work and craftsmanship required for this, it is not surprising that haute couture models are so expensive.
>> A couture collection is modelled in toile and finished off down to every detail so that the final result can clearly be seen. The buttons are covered with toile so that their relationship vis à vis the garment can be assessed. Pocket flaps and other details are also attached for the same reason. A pattern can be reproduced in advance on toile so that the modelling can be done on the basis of the pattern's effect. As soon as the toile is ready it is measured on a model and changes are made and registered on the toile. On a jacket, for example, the correct length is indicated or the form of a collar corrected. The toiliste then knows exactly which changes have to be made to the toile. The toile is then taken apart and a new example is made. These processes are repeated until the toile looks perfect. After fitting for the last time, the toile is completely taken apart and the pattern parts are traced onto paper or cardboard, from which the definitive model is cut in the appropriate fabric.

This labour-intensive process is much too expensive for mass-produced, ready-to-wear garments. For this reason it may even sometimes be left out, but generally a highly simplified version is used. The clothing industry bases its pattern designs on impersonal, average measurements and standard calculations; smaller and larger sizes are done according to mathematical formulae. Drapings are used here to develop and try out new ideas and forms. With more exclusive labels a basic pattern is used to model new forms. The model is then adjusted and altered on a dress stand. Finally, a sample of this is made from the definitive or a similar fabric.
>> There are also specialised firms where the manufacturer of ready-to-wear clothing can purchase toiles. The toile is taken apart in the factory and a pattern made from it. Just like ordinary paper patterns, toile patterns can be made in larger or smaller sizes.

Karin Schacknat

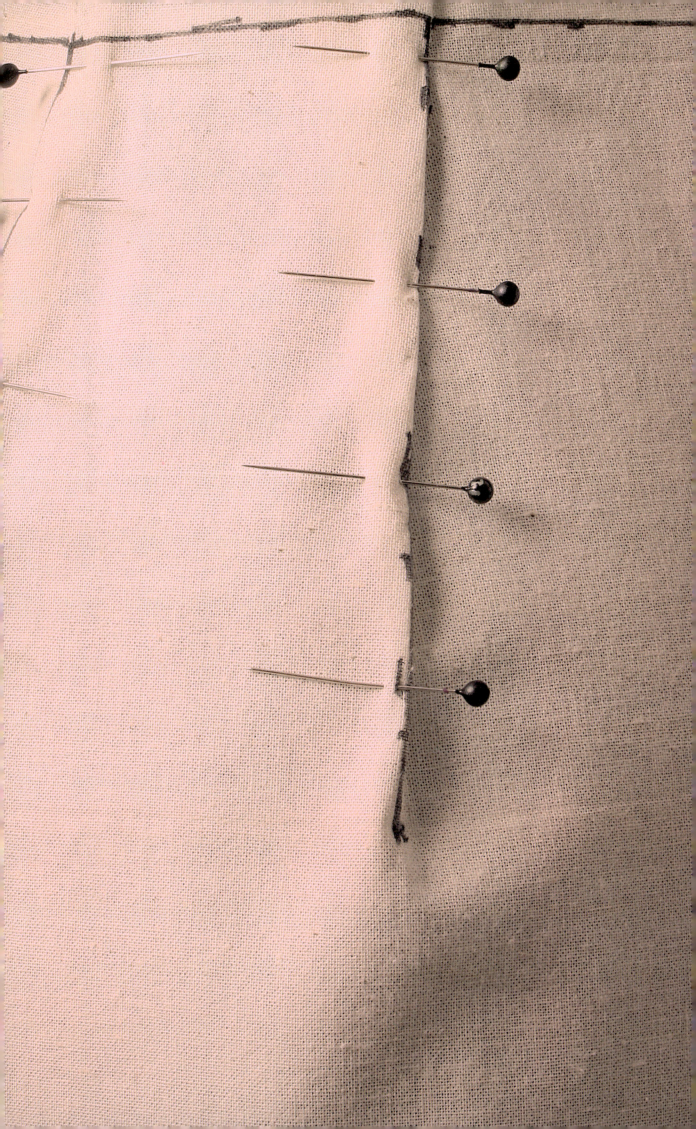

Eduard van Rijn

Comments from the field of practice

Draping continues to be practised behind the scenes of the contemporary fashion world. The degree to which this happens has to do with the quality and exclusivity of the end product, as well as with the type of garment: new patterns for menswear are generally derived from already existing patterns and draping is hardly ever used. Draping is almost exclusively used for women's collections.
>> I recently talked with five people representing different segments of the profession. All five make toiles at an advanced level. The separate accounts of these interviews are reproduced below in abridged form. Even though this may not result in a complete picture it does provide a certain indication concerning the vicissitudes of draping in contemporary fashion production.
>> Despite the different backgrounds of the interviewees, there are certain similarities in their views. They all agree, for example, that the prevailing system of draping, which dates from the first half of the twentieth century, is utterly impervious to modernisation. It was good right from the start and it still cannot be bettered.
>> What was also surprising was that all those concerned showed a lot of enthusiasm for their profession and for the discipline of draping in particular. There was no sign of the familiar preconception that draping is 'boring' and 'stuffy'. In any case, those guilty of such a negative viewpoint have usually never been involved with draping anyway.
>> I would have liked very much to talk to Hieron Pessers (1939-2004) but he unfortunately passed away a few years ago. In addition to being an artist, he taught draping techniques, having learned the craft with Givenchy in Paris. He later worked for an haute couture house in Rome. Hieron taught in the fashion departments of art academies and other institutes in London, Tokyo, Antwerp and various places in the Netherlands. He must have been a fantastic teacher, as well as an authority in his field. His name was mentioned by several of the interviewees, and always with a great deal of respect. His influence on the development of the discipline among the younger generation should not be underestimated.

> Eduard van Rijn

He currently lives a withdrawn life, occasionally, however, he still receives clients. Eduard van Rijn is a couturier of the old school, and as such he has had an eventful life.
>> After his finals at the fashion department of the Rotterdam art academy in 1956, he immediately gave a show. *'But it was all very lumpish then. I had absolutely no technical experience.'* Nevertheless, he had already started making hats. He drew the attention of Tina Onassis (*'a cousin of the great Onassis'*) who enticed him to Greece where he produced clothes for a number of wealthy shipowners' wives. *'I had a luxurious life, but I was a sort of prisoner. Always working, I never got away. After a year and a half I had enough of it.'*
>> Then he met Machteld, the wife of Karel Appel and the muse of Balenciaga. She advised him to apply for a job with Balenciaga and shortly afterwards he was taken on as toiliste. It was very instructive to see the master at work. *'He was a man of eyes and hands. He worked for the rulers of the world, for the wives of NATO authorities, for example. And Marlene Dietrich was close to him for a while. When we were having our midday lunch outside and we'd see the Dior folk going by - they used to work in the vicinity - we always found that much too vulgar.'*
>> A year later he returned to the Netherlands where he worked for private customers. In the meantime, his awareness of quality and skills in the area of draping had progressed and in the 1970s he started teaching at the Charles Montaigne school of couture. *'I once presented entire collections in toile in the show for the final presentation. I've never ceased going in new directions instead of conventional ones.'*
>> Eduard van Rijn approaches the profession like a sculptor: *'Creating a form is wonderful! Most people are unable to do it, forming and seeing at the same time like an architect. The difficult thing is suggesting space. Feeling where it has to be cut with the grain and where on the bias.'* In 1989 he published the manual Mouleren & Draperen [Modelling & Draping]. A few years earlier he had started a private school in Arnhem, the École de Couture. In 1987 he wrote a letter to President Gorbatsjov. *'We were the first school to seek contact with Russia when perestroika became a household word.'* This resulted in an invitation and a joint show with students from the fashion department of the University of Moscow. *'There was an engineering course in pattern drawing. But they couldn't make toiles there.'*

2 CONTEMPORARY
DESIGNERS
20 - 2**1**

Comments from the field of practice:
> Martin van
* Dusseldorp*

Martin van Dusseldorp for Viktor & Rolf

>> The École de Couture was granted only a short life. After a few years Eduard van Rijn had to close his school when subsidy was withdrawn. But his skills had not gone unnoticed in Moscow, where he presented a show of his own for the new rich. However, *'No foreigners came to have a look, only Russian maffiosi. But by the end of the evening everything was sold out.'*

>> A business relationship with a Russian manufacturer blossomed. *'I was given a flat in Moscow and carte blanche financially. Then a building in Paris was bought up, which used to be Dior's fur shop, with staff and everything. I was supposed to immediately make a collection for it, and there had to be a clear Russian air to it. Fur, amber... The customers were French, South Americans, Saudis, Italian aristocracy. I also designed something for ex-Empress Soraya. I was spending three months in Moscow and three weeks in Paris. But it didn't go well. It turned out that no income tax had been paid for four years. The whole thing was confiscated. A dreadful disgrace!'*

>> And so Eduard van Rijn returned again to The Hague where he created clothes for a select clientele, particularly evening and wedding dresses, including Princess Margarita's wedding dress.

>> He almost never drew his designs, but draped straight away. *'I know the direction I want to go in, but you have to let the fabric go its own way. It will show you what has to be done. The law of gravity remains in effect whatever the case: from up to down.'*

> Martin van Dusseldorp

Each season the fashion press devotes attention to the latest collection by Viktor & Rolf, their show and the appearance of the iconic bespectacled duo themselves. In fact there is a third man - invisible but important: Martin van Dusseldorp, their toiliste and technical jack-of-all-trades. He avoids the spotlight, preferring to operate behind the scenes. *'I've actually got the nicest job!'* he says.

>> In the distant past Martin van Dusseldorp studied dress-making and clothing manufacture at the MTS Utrecht. He did not learn draping there, but did it on his own. At the age of twenty-one he was head of an atelier making curtains. *'But that wasn't what I wanted. I was sort of idealistic and wanted to help young designers who usually have little idea of pattern making, draping and things like that. In the early 90s I came in contact with Orson & Bodil, Saskia van Drimmelen and other newcomers at the time. They could all use technical help. In addition I was working for the theatre world. When I was approached by Viktor and Rolf in the mid-90s I had to refuse at first - I was simply too busy.'*

>> He now works exclusively for them. Did the two of them know much about technique? *'Oh yes, certainly. Although you can't see their individual contributions in isolation. The mutual chemistry is perfect.'*

>> Toiles are usually made at full scale since then it becomes clear how something falls in its actual proportions. The production of a garment is preceded by an extensive process of choices and considerations until the final product satisfies everyone's wishes. Viktor & Rolf supply ideas on paper, sometimes putting them in fabric on the dummy. Martin van Dusseldorp, accustomed to their hand, starts work on the ideas, draping on the basis of an approximate, rough pattern. A discussion is held about the initial result and on the basis of that a trial model is then executed in toile. This is followed by another discussion. The design (possibly changed) is now instigated and the final creation is carried out step by step in close collaboration and with more and more refinements.

>> All of this takes place in a relaxed atmosphere, based on mutual trust. Martin van Dusseldorp does not reject any of Viktor & Rolf's assignments - for him impossibilities are a challenge. He has gradually gained greater and greater responsibilities and has supported their exhibitions in word and deed, including those in Boston and Paris.

>> The moment when the collection is ready, however, is not a cause for celebration. *'To begin with, I can never take distance from the products. Nor am I pleased when something is finished. The show is always a really emotional moment - for all of us. Only later, when you see the clothes at an exhibition, for example, do you look at them differently. Then you see them perhaps presented in the same domain as, say, Chanel, and then you think, well, we're definitely a match for that. Hey, that's great, we really worked hard!'*

>> And sometime you have to take distance. *'There was once an exhibition in the museum in Groningen. I looked at the display with one of our garments and saw that there was something wrong with it. My natural reaction was to want to correct it on the spot, but I was immediately stopped by the attendant.'*

>> Martin van Dusseldorp is a perfectionist. This is also shown by his personal preferences, which are not exclusively focussed on the old masters - Balenciaga, Givenchy - but also on the finer points of the craft in a wider sense, *'such as 18th century embroidery, or how sometimes a lining or smocking has been beautifully used. Other times you see old clothing exhibited, where the cut still displays certain teething troubles. And conversely, with a costume film in which everything fits perfectly, I think, no, that's not right. How would it be if they made these film costumes with the same badly-fitting jacket backs, the way they really were?'*

>> This perfectionism means that Martin van Dusseldorp keeps experiencing nasty moments. *'There are certain things that make their first appearance on the catwalk that make my heart miss a beat. Like that wedding dress fringed with Swarovski crystals. Imagine the model getting her foot stuck in it and stumbling. Awful! I also had such a terrible moment with the jacket with that collar like a bed pillow, with the model's hair spread out on it as though she was asleep. It looked very light, but in reality it was a heavy construction.'*

Comments from the field of practice:

> *Tim van
Steenbergen*

Tim van Steenbergen, Red Star Line collection, spring - summer 2007. Photo: Etienne Tordoir, Katrijn van Giel

>> Clearly, V & R's house toiliste has to be able to do more than just perfect draping. He is also a sort of alchemist. *'The Silver Collection, for example, involved a whole load of things. The linings had to be made hard and this required all sorts of chemical processes. A lot had to be invented for the sake of certain effects, such as the foundation and the preparation of the cloth. This was simply ordinary cotton, but it had to be waxed in advance, and then etamine and lacquer were applied, and here and there some welding to make the skirt more stable. The bodice is made of milliner's gauze, but this goes limp as soon as it gets damp. So we soaked it first in acid, then coppered it and finally plated it with silver. As a matter of fact, we also make the masks and all sorts of other accessories here in house. Sometimes in this profession you also need to know how to use a hammer and saw.'*

>> Is there any advice he would give to prospective designers? *'Actually more of a wish than a piece of advice - that people should be more passionate about what they do. I miss the passion sometimes; everything has to be crammed in as quickly as possible. Surely it's all about inspiration!'*

> *Tim van Steenbergen*

'The lessons by Hieron Pessers opened a whole world for me. The contact with him was the most significant thing that had happened to me for years. It had an enormous influence on my creativity,' answers the Belgian designer Tim van Steenbergen in reply to my question about a specific personal experience in connection with his professional field.

>> It was in the third year of his studies in the department of fashion at the art academy in Antwerp that he was taught specific, traditional draping techniques by Pessers. This led him to discover the leitmotif in his own way of working. Success was not long in coming. Not yet thirty, Tim van Steenbergen has already had about twenty professional shows (most of them in Paris), in addition to numerous exhibitions and projects, such as the costumes for the production *D'un soir un jour* by the Rosas dance group. His ready-to-wear collections are praised by the press and the public for their nonchalant grace.

>> One of the designer's important basic principles is that *'Clothing should be wearable. The design should never dominate, but always serve the person wearing it.'*

>> Each of his collection requires a lot of draping, which is done exactly according to the guidelines used in haute couture in the 1950s and 60s. Tim van Steenbergen drapes himself, and does it with dedication. Draping serves him on the one hand as a technical aid in realising a design sketch, but on the other hand it is an indispensable part of the design process itself. *'You need guts to keep working constantly on form. I once worked for five days on just one draping. Seven days even when I was at the academy! At any rate, it's interesting to keep persevering. It's my passion.'*

>> The draped stage is what he loves the most in the whole process of creating a collection. *'The nicest thing is the construction of the garment, especially when you find the form you're looking for. That's what it's all about, not the subsequent glamour!'*

>> And the most difficult thing with drapings? *'The sleeve! It's very difficult to construct a good sleeve in a classical way.'* That's why every trainee that we have here has to learn it. I always hope that they understand how important it is.' He is zealous in encouraging fashion students in general: *'Do it! Learn it! It's your baggage. You have to know where you want your work to go. You have to know what you're drawing. And draping is the technique. The element of craft adds extra value to your products, and you need that to carry on. There is so much competition... and traditional values are precisely what a lot of buyers are looking for.'*

>> Tim van Steenbergen takes his examples in the fashion trade from the line of famous haute couture masters. *'The Balenciaga of old, Yves Saint Laurent, Dior too. I can look at these every week.'* Other names he mentions are Vionnet and Grès.

>> In fashion at the moment we can see a certain penchant for elements from the haute couture of the 1950s and 60s. He sees this as a reaction to industrial mass production. *'People are looking for something authentic, something to distinguish themselves, something that has a special warmth.'*

>> This sort of warmth is time-consuming and therefore expensive. How can this be reconciled with the rejection of exclusivity that Tim van Steenbergen embraces as a principle? *'Only the first part of the process, the draping, is exclusive. But then a pattern is derived from it so that the garment can be serially produced. No, it's not cheap, but it is at least accessible.'*

Comments from the field of practice:

> *Michiel Keuper*
> *Els Roseboom*

Keupr/van Bentm, Twist 2000. Photo: Peter Stigter

> Michiel Keuper

He is the 'Keupr' part of the sensational label Keupr/VanBentm that he started with Francisco van Benthum, a former fellow student at the Arnhem Art Academy in 1993. Michiel Keuper has worked as a designer for the label Ghost, for the designers duo Suzanne Clements and the Brazilian Inácio Ribeiro in London, for Orson & Bodil and for Puma. He currently lives and works in Berlin.

>> He discovered the art of draping about two years after his fashion studies. *'I immediately saw something in it when attending a course in draping with Rixt van der Tol. Later I followed another course with Hieron Pessers, a master of draping who saw it purely as a technique for making a three-dimensional realisation of a particular sketch. But for me draping became a key to finding a design. You can compare draping with modelling in clay. Because you're directly working three-dimensionally, you come up with ideas that you would never have been able to think up on paper. And it is very concrete: everything you can do on a dummy you can also do in reality. You also see the proportions immediately. How wide a waistband should actually be, for example. On paper these sorts of things are often unclear.'*

>> After Hieron Pessers's unexpected death, Michiel Keuper was asked to give lessons in moulage for the masters course in the department of fashion in Arnhem. *'Actually I hesitated, because I felt that I still had too little experience. But there was simply nobody else at the time, and if nobody teaches it, then such a discipline dies out.'*

>> So he took on the challenge. And with success. *'Since then I've gained a lot of experience in teaching draping. For many students from elsewhere this was an unknown field - draping is by no means a self-evident part of all fashion studies.'*

>> Michiel Keuper works systematically step by step: first the cloth and the tailor's dummy are prepared, and then the students venture successively on a straight and a flared skirt, a toile de corps or basic bodice, and a corset with stays (*'indispensable as a structural foundation in couture'*). Then they are allowed to choose a photograph and model a copy of what they see. *'In this way you're forced to find solutions. There can be no excuses, like, oh well, it's also OK without sleeves.'* The lessons finally lead to draping one's own designs. How long does it take to master draping? *'You can certainly learn the basics in a couple of weeks. But the refinement, the subtleties, that takes much longer!'*

>> Michiel Keuper has a weakness for haute couture production. *'There you have much more independence than when you work on commission. But the traditional system of haute couture is out-of-date. I'd like to try and find a contemporary form for it - working on designs in a limited edition, perhaps an emphasis on special details, things like that.'*

>> And the drapings? *'They extend the possibilities of the design process, and will continue to do so. My advice would be: create your own freedom in it!'*

> Els Roseboom

Her business is located in the Jordaan district of Amsterdam, in a polygonal building that used to house a ballet school. Here she lives and works, the living quarters shrinking as the working part keeps expanding. Long skylights let in light, which is useful for pattern drawing. Now, three and a half years after graduating from the fashion department of the Arnhem art academy, she runs a business with seven employees making toiles and patterns for various clients.

>> That was not what she actually envisaged when she was still a student. *'I wanted of course to become a fashion designer, which still has the most prestige among students. Making toiles and patterns is often a job that is undervalued. You don't become a star, but remain in the background. Some people look down on you enormously - is that what you're doing?!'*

>> Nevertheless, the technical side seemed to be very attractive. *'I was always busy looking for solutions, for ways to make clothes differently than in the conventional manner. Not freaky stuff, though, but wearable clothing that can be produced serially - and to see how far you can go in this. That was the challenge for me. I had already regularly done this sort of work, in Antwerp, in addition to my studies in Arnhem. The head teacher didn't allow it because I was missing too many lessons, but I did it anyway.'*

>> There turned out to be more and more good sides to the discipline she had chosen. *'I do like the atmosphere behind the scenes. Working in a team, all of you enthusiastic about something, and being part of a greater whole. And then the excitement before the show. Sometimes I would be sitting in the bus still sewing the night before. I saw an awful lot of shows then and got to know a lot of people. Dries van Noten, Walter van Beirendonck... in the meantime I've built up a whole network.'*

>> After her studies Els Roseboom further developed her discipline and now there's nothing she would rather be doing.

>> There are only a few specialised firms in this branch of the fashion industry. All manner of different clients - *'the better producers of ready-to-wear clothing and designers'* - know where to find her. *'I always get the somewhat complicated cases. Big commercial companies don't make trial models from their simple patterns but send them straight to China for processing. Yet a lot of manufacturers there are abandoning this - it takes too long till something is done well.'*

>> There's no shortage of work. She can allow herself to choose the most attractive assignments and to turn down others. What is attractive? *'Carrying out designs for special garments, like the big concluding dress for Oscar Suleyman's show. But pleasant collaboration is also important. If I have annoying experiences with a client then I don't take on any more work for them.'*

>> Els Roseboom receives sketches from her clients, on the basis of which she has to make a toile, resulting finally in a

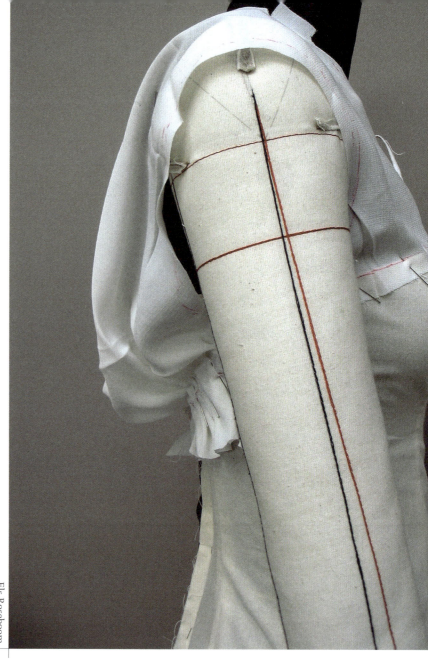

Els Roseboom

usable pattern. *'Sometimes I'm given a basic pattern as well, but usually I use my own so that I'm more or less working with the relevant size. I drape a lot of details: pieces of the underside of the sleeve, for example.'* After the work is done the client receives, if desired, a copy of the finished pattern; the original remains in the firm's archive.

>> A few months ago Els Roseboom acquired an advanced computer system with a special table for scanning the hand-drawn pattern at certain points. The pattern parts then appear perfectly outlined on the screen where they can be elaborated further. The width of the fabric has to be inputted since laying the fabric is also done digitally. The finished pattern is trans-ferred to a plotter and printed out onto special self-adhesive paper which is ironed onto the fabric. The pattern can then be cut out without the use of a single pin. *'The computer system does not make the work any easier,'* Els Roseboom explains, *'because you have to be able to deal with all the digital hassles. But it saves an enormous amount of time. Increasing and reducing sizes is all done by the computer. Or if something has to be traced then it's done in the wink of an eye instead of needing many hours work.'*

>> Els Roseboom also trains people, *'with the idea perhaps that they'll stay with the firm.'* Instead of expanding even further, she would rather deepen her professional knowledge and experience. And the future? *'Rosy! It seems to me that there are more and more labels, and more and more collections each year. And there is still no system of production other than this one.'*

Karin Schacknat

3 PREPARATIONS FOR DRAPING

REQUIREMENTS

Dress stands > **0001** > In the mid-19th century there was a flourishing dress stand industry in Paris. At present we can only recognise a few of the names of these old firms, such as Stockman. **>>** The very first shop-window dummies date from 1797 and were made of wicker woven like an open basket in the form of a male or female figure.

0001

0002

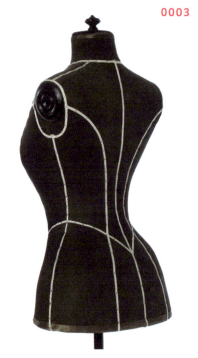

0003

> **0002 / 0003** > In the early 1840s these were replaced by figures made of iron wire. The dress stand that could be worked on made its appearance in 1848. Likewise made of wicker, it was covered with a layer of cotton waste or horsehair and then upholstered with linen. **>>** In 1880 people started to use dress stands made of papier-maché covered with linen.

0004

0005

> **0004 / 0005** > The French call it a 'buste-mannequin'. A dress stand with an adjustable centre front and centre back is not suitable for draping, since these are the most important points for draping, given that usually only a half model is made. **>>** A dress stand should be sturdy and preferably stand on a metal foot; a wooden foot is less stable. **>>** There are dress stands with and without shoulders.

>> The advantage of a stand with shoulders is that shoulder pads stay firmly anchored and it is easy to see whether a sleeve has been pinned too tightly. >> There are also dress stands for trousers, bathing suits and skirts, as well as half-scale dress stands for trying out experimental forms.
>> It is sometimes possible to find an old dress stand at an auction or a market, often beautifully formed, but very dated because of the changes that the human figure has gone through. Such an old-fashioned stand is nice as a curiosity but unsuitable for draping contemporary garments. People today are taller and more robust than in earlier centuries. Fashion through the ages has featured an ideal image of the body, to which the dress stand industry has adapted itself.

>> Pay attention to the following points when purchasing a dress stand: >> Modern proportions. >> Covering suitable for sticking pins into. >> A correct body length. >> Bust, waist and hip size should not deviate too much from the measurements you need. Bust is the most important measurement. It is better that the dimensions of the stand are a little smaller than the required measurements. How you can adjust the stand to your own measurements is dealt with on pp. 36-37.

Fabric > The fabric used for draping is called 'toile'. In the past a fine, soft cotton muslin in various thicknesses was used. >> Nowadays we use unbleached cotton which is also available in different thicknesses. >> Draping is done with a toile that corresponds as much as possible to the thickness of the fabric in which the final product will be produced. >> If the toile is not wide enough, a piece in the same grain can be attached. >> Draping in couture is sometimes done in the definitive fabric because of the right sturdiness and fall. This is done in cases where the definitive fabric deviates too much from the toile, as with a tricot for example.

0006

> **0006** > **Selvedge** > these are the edges on the two sides of the fabric so woven and finished that they cannot unravel. **Lengthwise grain** > This runs along the length of the fabric, in the same direction as the warp threads of the loom. **Crosswise grain** > This runs from selvedge to selvedge. These threads are usually weaker than the warp threads. **True Bias** > An angle of 45° drawn on the selvedge is the true bias. The bias is very important for draping. The fabric is at its most flexible on the true bias and takes on the form of the body well. It also falls more easily, especially when the fabric is gathered. Gathers in the lengthwise or crosswise grain look stiffer and stand out more. >> It is advisable to be accurate in dealing with the straight or bias grain and with the specific possibilities that fabric prepared on the bias offers.

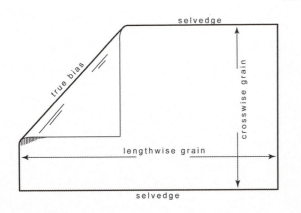

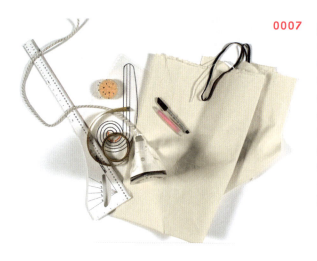

0007 **Equipment and workspace > Workspace > 0007 >** Sufficient room for the dress stand. **>>** Large cutting table. **Dress stand > Toile >** Select for draping the quality of toile that is similar to the final garment. **Ironing board and steam iron > Dressmaker's scissors >** With sharp points. **Pins >** Fine and long. **Black and red fineliner or ballpoint pen >** Black for marking off details on the fabric, red for indicating the grain. **Tape measure > Dressmaker's ruler > French curve >** This is a curve used for drawing arm holes, neckline and small roundings **White and black tape >** For indicating lines and markings on the dress stand and the toile.

PREPARATIONS

Measurements > Begin with measuring when you are going to make a toile for someone. The most accurate way is to take measurements over the underwear. Secure a tape around the waist and press it down to the narrowest part of the upper part of the body; now the waist is clearly visible. **>>** The person being measured should stand upright and not hold their breath!

Measuring the body

> **0008 > BW = Bust >** Measure around the fullest part of the bust. Make sure that the tape measure is held horizontally at the back so the shoulder blades are included.
WW = Waist > Measure around the waist band. Hold one finger in between and breathe out. **HW = Hip >** Measure around the fullest part of the bottom, standing with the feet together. With heavy thighs the fullest part will lie lower. **HH = Hip height >** Hold the tape measure around the fullest part (HW) and measure the height from the waistband to the tape measure. **NW = Neck width >** Measure loosely around the neck, allowing the tape measure to rest on the shoulders. **FCW = Front chest width >** Measure the front from armhole to armhole.
> **0009 > BL = Back length >** Measure the centre back from the prominent neck bone to the waistband. **BAW = Back width >** Measure the back from armhole to armhole. **SW = Shoulder width >** Measure along the top of the shoulder from the neck to the most prominent part of the shoulder bone.
> **0010 > BD = Bust depth >** Measure at the front from the point where the neck meets the shoulder to the tip of the bust. **FL = Front length >** Measure at the front from the point where the neck meets the shoulder, across the bust to the waistband.

0008

0009

0010

sleeve and arm

> Measurements for trousers and leg

Preparations:
> Measurements
> Measuring the body
> Measurements for

> Equipment and workspace

Requirements:

3 PREPARATIONS FOR DRAPING

32 - 33

Measurements for sleeve and arm > 0011 / 0012 > **UAW = Upper arm width** > Measure the fullest part of the upper arm (biceps). **EW = Elbow width** > Measure around the thickest part of the elbow, with the arm in a slightly bent and relaxed position. **WC = Wrist circumference** > Measure around the wrist. **AL = Arm length** > Measure from the shoulder bone across a slightly bent elbow to the wrist bone. **LAL = Lower arm length** > Measure from the elbow to the wrist bone. **AHC = Arm hole circumference** > Measure from the shoulder bone, under the arm and back to the shoulder bone.

0011

0012

0013

Measurements for trousers and leg > 0013 > **WW = Waist** > Measure around the waist band. Hold one finger in between and breathe out. **HW = Hip** > Measure around the fullest part of the bottom, standing with feet together. With heavy thighs the fullest part will lie lower. **HH = Hip heigt** > Hold the tape measure around the fullest part (HW) and measure the height from the waistband to the tape measure. **CD = Crutch depth** > Have the model sit on a flat surface. Measure down the side from the waistband to the flat surface. This distance + 1 cm is the crutch depth. **SL = Side length (also known as outside leg length)** > Measure down the side from the waistband to the ground, without shoes. **LL = Leg length** > This is the side length minus the crutch depth.

KH = Knee height > Measure on the side from the ground to the fullest past of the knee. **ULW = Upper leg width** > Measure across the fullest part of the upper leg. **KW = Knee width** > Measure across the thickest part of the knee. **FW = Foot width** > Measure around the foot across the heel and instep.

>> The following table of measurements is based on a body height of 1 m 70 cm and is not absolute. >> Tables of measurements are based on average body measurements and will differ according to the type of figure.

Preparations:
> Measurements
> Measuring the body
> Measurements for sleeve and arm
> Measurements for trousers and leg
> Table of measurements
> Preparing the dress stand

Standard sizes – Measurements of the dress stand – Wearer's size

Size		36	38	40	42	Wearer's size
BW	Bust	84	88	92	96	...
WW	Waist	64	68	72	76	...
HW	Hip	94	98	102	106	...
HH	Hip height	20	21	22	22	...
BL	Back length	41	41	41	41	...
BAW	Back width	34	35	36	37	...
SW	Shoulder width	12	12.2	12.4	12.6	...
NW	Neck width	36	37	38	39	...
BD	Bust depth	25.5	25.8	26.1	27.4	...
FL	Front length	44.5	44.8	45.1	45.4	...
FCW	Front chest width	33	34	35	36	...

Sizes for arm and sleeve

		36	38	40	42	
UAW	Upper arm width	26	27	28	29	...
EW	Elbow width	22	23	24	25	...
WC	Wrist circumference	15	16	17	18	...
AL	Arm length	61	61	61	61	...
LAL	Lower arm length	25	25	25	25	...
AHC	Arm hole circumference	39	40	41	42	...

Sizes for trousers

		36	38	40	42	
WW	Waist	64	68	72	76	...
HW	Hip	94	98	102	106	...
HH	Hip height	20	21	22	22	...
CD	Crutch depth	25.5	26	26.5	27	...
SL	Side length	106	106	106	106	...
LL	Leg length	80.5	80	79.5	79	...
KH	Knee height	43	43	43	43	...
ULW	Upper leg width	53	54	55	56	...
KW	Knee width	36	37	38	39	...
FW	Foot width	29	30	31	32	...

0014

0015

0016

Preparing the dress stand > Placing the permanent demarcation lines on the dress stand > 0014 / 0015 / 0016 > Permanent demarcation lines are affixed to the dress stand. These lines correspond to the lines on the toile or can be transferred to the toile before it is removed from the dress stand. >> Use tape in a colour that contrasts with the dress stand. >> The permanent lines can be fixed to the dress stand with heavy-duty pins so that they can no longer shift. Place the tape on the stand and pin through the middle every 4-5 cm. >> With plastic dress stands the tapes are pinned onto the covering.

> 0014 / 0015 / 0016 / 0017 > Take hold of the covering right next to the tape and stick the pin through the middle of the tape, ensuring that the point of the pin is kept beneath the covering - do this with sewing pins without glass heads. When the pins are fixed in this way the tape can no longer shift position. **>>** The following permanent lines are placed on the stand.

1 Neck width (NW) > See table of measurements (34). Mark off this distance plus overlap onto the tape. Place the tape around the neck as low as possible in a nice curve. **2 Centre front (CF) >** Place the tape in the middle of the front going down from the neckline. Hang a pair of scissors on the tape so it can be affixed vertically.

3 Bust (BW) > Beginning at the centre front, place the tape around the fullest part of the bust. **>>** Ensure that the line remains horizontal at the back.

4 Waist (WW) > After measuring the front length from where the shoulder meets the neck and the back length from the prominent neck bone at the back of the neck, place the tape across these two points. **5 Centre back (CB) >** Divide the neck width and bust line in two, place pins on these points - this is the centre back. Hang a pair of scissors on the tape so it can be affixed vertically. Afterwards check whether the left and right halves are equal.

6 Hip height (HH) > Measure approx. 20-22 cm from the waistline down the side seam. At the centre front (CF) and centre back (CB) this distance will be somewhat shorter due to the curve of the hips. Make sure the tape is held horizontally. **7 Side seam >** The side seam lies midway between the CF and the CB. Divide the bust, waist and hip lines in two. Put pins on these points. The line will look better if the tape is placed 1 cm to the back.

> 0018 > 8 Shoulder point (on the outside) > Lay the measuring tape on the point where the side seam crosses the waist line and run it over the shoulder back to the same point. This distance halved is the shoulder point, which should be placed 1 cm to the back. **9 Shoulder line >** Divide the neckline from CF to CB into two equal parts. Place this point 1 cm to the back. Fix the tape to the shoulder.

10 Shoulder width (SW) > See table of measurements **>>** Look up the BW in the table and find the appropriate shoulder width. **11 Front chest width (FCW) >** See table of measurements **>>** Look up the BW in the table and find the appropriate front chest width. **12 Back width (BAW) >** See table of measurements **>>** Look up the BW in the table and find the appropriate back width. **13 Arm hole circumference (AHC) >** See table of measurements. **>>** Look up the BW in the table and find the appropriate arm hole circumference. **>>** Mark this distance plus overlap on the tape. Place the centre of the tape on the shoulder point and run the two ends across the chest line point and the back width line towards the side seam. Make sure the tape ends square to the side seam. Pin the tape in a nicely flowing line; an arm hole looks from the side like an egg slightly tilted backwards (centre of gravity to the fore). **>>** The dress stand is now ready for use.

0019 **Preparing the leg > permanent demarcation lines > 0019 / 0020 / 0021 >**
1 Waist (WW) > Place the tape on the narrowest part of the waist. Make sure the tape is kept horizontal. **2 Hip height (HH) >** Measure approx. 20-22 cm from the waistline down the side seam. At the centre front (CF) and centre back (CB) this distance will be somewhat shorter due to the curve of the hips. Make sure the tape is held horizontally. **3 Crutch depth (CD) >** Refer to the table of measurements on page 34. Mark the crutch depth on the side of the leg, down from the waist. Apply this line to the leg horizontally. **4 Knee height (KH) >** Place the tape around the fullest part of the knee. **5 Ankle >** Place the tape around the thinnest part of the leg. **6 Centre front / centre back (CF/CB) >** Place the tape in the centre and run it under the crutch to the back. Check that right and left are equal.
7 Balance line front and back > This line runs vertically from waist to foot along the middle of the front and back of the leg. **8 Side seam >** Divide the waist line and the HH line from CF to CB in two and put pins on these points. This is the side seam. Hang a pair of scissors on the tape so it can be affixed vertically.
9 Inside leg seam > Measure the upper leg and divide the distance in two. Mark off this distance from the side seam. This is the beginning of the inside leg seam. Divide the ankle into two and mark off this distance from the side seam. The tape runs straight down from the upper leg to the ankle. This is the inner leg seam.

0020

0021

0022

Shape lines > 0022 > Shape lines enable a particular form or line to be applied to a garment. These lines can be pinned onto the dress stand before draping or applied to the toile while the draping is in progress.

Adjusting the stand > Altering a standard dress stand. **>>** It is possible to apply small changes to a standard dress stand or to make it a little larger. **>>** Start by making a clear list of measurements of the dress stand. You can then add your own measurements to this list. This gives a clear indication of the places where the stand needs to be changed.

> 0023 > **Making the stand larger** > Use fibrefill for this. Determine where the extra padding has to come and pin or sew the fibrefill onto these places. Take care that the fibrefill forms a smooth contour with the stand. If several layers need to be applied, build them up layer by layer, using first a larger piece and then applying a smaller piece on top, so as to maintain a flowing contour. >> If necessary, use thin gauze for affixing the fibrefill. Sew the fibrefill and the gauze to the covering of the stand.

0023

> 0024 / 0025 > If the bust has to be increased, a brassiere can be placed on the stand and padded out with fibrefill. >> Use a strong piece of tricot to make a new covering for the stand in order to keep the fibrefill, gauze or brassiere in place. Pin two lengths of tricot tightly onto the stand along the neck, across the shoulder and on the side. >> Mark off the pinned line and stitch the seams. Turn the cover around and pull it onto the stand. Fasten the cover at the bottom and neck to the covering underneath. >> You can also use a tight-fitting T-shirt by fastening it to the bottom and neck of the stand. >> It is not possible, of course, to make a stand smaller. If a particular body size is smaller than that of the dress stand you will need to take account of this when producing the toile. >> You can also adapt the stand for other forms. You can use shoulder padding for special shoulder forms, for example, or expand the hips for a particular design.

0024

0025

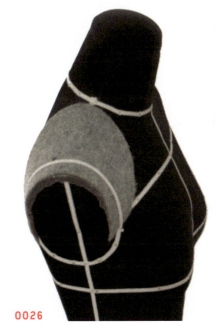

Shoulder pads > 0026 > If a garment has a padded shoulder then the padding is affixed to the dress stand before we start draping. For the correct form and thickness, choose a raglan padding for a raglan sleeve and a large, set in shoulder pad for a straight look. This shoulder pad will later be placed in the final garment. >> Pin the shoulder pad firmly to the stand. Pin tape around the shoulder where the arm hole appears.

0026

Requirements:
>> sturdy toile, 35 cm wide, 70 cm long
>> red, black and white sewing thread
>> fibrefill or other padding material
>> a piece of cardboard >> Take your own measurements or use standard sizes (see p. 34). The following example is based on a standard size 36.

(see p. 34)

Upper arm width	26
Elbow width	22
Wrist width	15
Arm length	61
Lower arm length	25
Arm hole circumference	39

>> Lay the carefully ironed piece of cloth on the table.

> Arm for stand with and without shoulders

0027

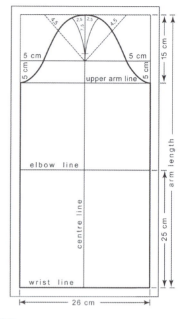

> **0028** > Use a pencil to draw a vertical line in the centre (centre line).
>> Draw the other lines on the fabric as in the example. >> Cut out the arm with a seam allowance of 1.5 cm.

0028

0029

> **0029 / 0030** > Pin the arm with the seam flat to the inside. This is the inside arm seam. Place the pinned seam in the centre of the fabric.

0030   **0031**

   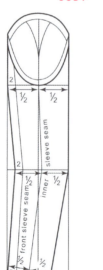

0032

0033

Inside arm > 0031 / 0032 > Lay the arm down flat with the seam facing up.
>> Go 2 cm in at the elbow line and plot the front arm line as shown in the example. >> Equidistant from this line draw a second line at a distance of 2 cm (= front sleeve seam) >> Mark off the half wrist width at the bottom and use a set square to plot the back of the arm, as shown in the example.
>> Divide the wrist width, elbow width and upper arm width in two. >> Plot the under sleeve seam across these points. **Outside arm > 0033 >** Turn over the pinned piece of cloth. >> Go in 2 cm at the elbow line and draw the front arm line on this side too. >> Here too the wrist width is marked off and the back of the arm plotted with a set square. >> Divide the wrist, elbow and upper arm widths in two and >> plot the upper sleeve seam as shown in the example.

Preparations:

0034

> **0034** > Fold the arm open. >> Machine stitch (at least twice) the grain lines (dotted lines) in red. >> Stitch the seam lines (line of dots or dashes) in black at least twice.

> **0035** > A choice is now made for a right or a left arm, depending on one's work preference. >> Stitch the inside seam and stitch along the curved sections. >> Cut the arm out with seam allowance, using scissors to make an incision for the elbow line on the front as far as the seam. >> Sew the dart at the top of the arm closed. >> Take a rolled up piece of fibrefill, tie a cord around it and pull the roll through the arm. (Take care not to overstuff.)

Arm hole cardboard > **0036** > Measure the diameter of the arm hole on the stand at its widest point. >> Mark off this line minus 1 cm on the cardboard, as shown in the example. A-B = arm hole diameter. Draw a vertical line through the centre. Make the form of an armhole by forming an oval with the measuring tape, with the circumference of the arm hole minus 2 cm (= here 37 cm). >> Draw the oval and cut out the arm hole cardboard.

Wrist cardboard > **0037** > Use the measuring tape to make an oval the same size as the wrist and draw this onto the cardboard. >> Cut out the wrist oval. >> Both ovals are covered with toile. >> The wrist cardboard is firmly affixed to the bottom of the arm. Take care that the wrist cardboard is attached in the correct direction. >> Sew the arm hole cardboard into the top of the arm. >> Sew, if desired, bands onto the arm, or a shoulder piece, so you can pin the arm to the dress stand while working.

0035

0036

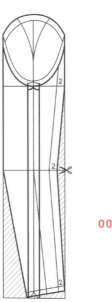

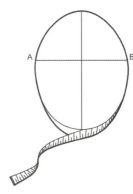

0037

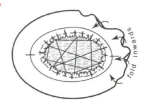

Arm for stand with shoulders > **0038 / 0039 / 0040** > See the instructions for a dress stand without shoulders. Do not close the dart at the top of the arm. Fill the arm to a slightly lesser height, double fold in the top of the arm and sew the semi-circle to the inside.

0038

0039

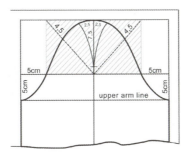

0040

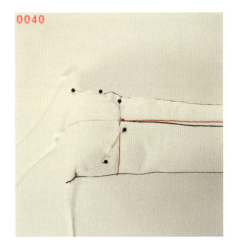

> Preparing the toile
> Sequence of work
> Extra width table
> Ten golden rules

Preparations:

Preparing the toile > 0041 > The toile needs some preparation before it can be used. **Straightening the fabric >** Since toile is wrapped somewhat crookedly on the roll in the factory, it first has to be straightened. Do this by pulling the toile in the opposite direction. The finer the make-up of the fabric, the straighter it is and stretching is not necessary. **Iron the toile >** Before starting work the toile has to be ironed, preferably with a steam iron, so that the final result is not influenced by wrinkles and folds. Because of the material's finish, take care not to iron the toile with too much heat or dampness. **Applying lines onto the toile >** In earlier times, these lines were applied in the following manner: a thread was drawn from the toile every 10 cm in the length and breadth and a red thread inserted instead, so that it was easy to see how the grain ran during the draping. This can be seen in the old toiles made by Elsa Schiaparelli (1890-1973), which are still sometimes to be seen in exhibitions in Paris. They show the 10 by 10 cm panels, as well as stamps at various places, which she made to indicate that the detail was well modelled. If the detail had no stamp then the toiliste had to model it again.

>> A toiliste would thus begin with pulling out threads and re-threading the toile, and collecting the pins from the floor. >> In order to save time, these lines are nowadays applied to the fabric with a pen. This should be done carefully in order to achieve a good result. The more carefully you work with a perfectly straight grain, the faster you will master the technique.

0041

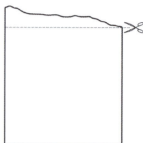

Sequence of work > 0042 > The toile is prepared as follows. >> For a symmetrical model, a half toile is modelled, from centre front (CF) to centre back (CB). Always allow for a 4 cm seam on the CF and the CB so that the toile can be well fastened to the stand. >> Should you later want to make a whole toile for fitting, then you have sufficient seam allowance. >> For an asymmetrical model, a whole toile is modelled, so that the path of the lines can easily be judged. >> For modelled garments a whole toile first has to be made. >> Place the CF and CB line in the middle of the fabric, model one half and mark this off. >> Pull the lines straight on the table along a ruler or French curve. >> Fold the toile double at CF and CB and copy (mirror) the lines onto the other side. >> In the case of a half modelled toile, a second half can of course be taken up and sewn on at CF and CB.

0042

0043

Marking > 0043 > Make a black line where there are pins or where a demarcation line has been pinned, so you can see what the pattern parts are. >> Control points (points where pattern parts have to be adjoined) are also marked off. >> After you have removed the toile from the stand, these little marks are drawn into nice flowing and taut lines with a ruler or French curve. >> Marking should be done systematically - while it may seem self-evident with simple pieces, with complicated toiles it is important not to forget anything. >> To be on the safe side, centre front and centre back can also be marked.

Extra width and making note of seams > With a modelled garment the seams are pinned to the outside. If you put the toile together with the seams facing inwards, you will not have enough space. >> For the sake of freedom of movement the extra width now has to be marked at a number of points. >> Watch out: these are extra widths for a half pattern; the amount noted in the side seam will later be twice that amount for the whole panel. >> Plot the extra widths as you see fit; these depend on the final design.

Front chest width	0.75	1	1.25	1
Back width	1	1.25	1.5	1.75
Waist	according to the design			
Hip	according to the design			

Arm hole

Shoulder point	0.25	0.5	0.75	1
Deepening	1.5	2.5	3.5	4.5
Side seam	1	2	3	4

Deepening the neck, for a rounded neck

CF	0.5	0.75	1	1
Shoulder	0.5	0.75	0.75	1
CB	0.25	0.5	0.5	0.5

> Never deepen the CB neck more than 1 cm.

0044

Seam allowance > 0044 > Draw 1 cm seam allowance on all pattern parts. >> Pinning together flat: The seams and darts are pinned together flat so the model can be checked on the dress stand. >> The one seam allowance is folded over, laid over the other and pinned (or basted) on top of the seam allowance with the lines facing out. >> The model thus immediately hangs nicely and you can easily see if everything (form, fall, lines, seams and details) has been done correctly. **Checking >** When the toile on the stand has been checked and corrected where necessary, the model is taken apart and the pattern parts are cut clean. **Clean cutting >** You do this when you are going to produce the pattern in the final fabric or use it for a new toile. Clean cutting means the seam allowance is cut from the toile. Make sure all demarcation lines, control points and grain lines are indicated on the toile. >> If necessary you can spray the pattern parts with starch to make them easier to work with.

TEN GOLDEN RULES FOR DRAPING

1 >> Always prepare the toile (unbleached cotton) by indicating sufficient horizontal and vertical grain with red marker pen. **2 >>** Always place the toile on the dress stand with a purely straight grain or on the true bias. **3 >>** Pin the toile onto the covering of the stand, stick the pin into the covering and back again so that the toile cannot shift. **4 >>** As soon as the toile does not do what you want it to do or the dress stand seems to get in the way, then CUT! **5 >>** Do not be too economical with cutting; a new piece of toile can always be pinned on. **6 >>** For seams and darts always pin the layers of fabric TOGETHER, for pleats OVER each other. **7 >>** Carefully mark off the pinned toile with a black pen or fineliner and provide enough control points. **8 >>** Always carefully touch up the marked off lines on a table (with a ruler) into whole pattern parts. **9 >>** Check the toile by cutting it out (with a seam allowance of 1 cm) and pinning or basting it in the draping manner (one seam folded in over the other and with the lines on the outside). **10 >>** Turn the toile (corrected if necessary) into a complete pattern by cutting it 'clean' (without seams) and transferring it to paper. (Do not forget to check the measurements of the pattern parts.)

4 SKIRTS

BASIC FORMS

Straight skirt > Preparing the toile

> **0045** > Prepare the toile as shown in the example. >> Length: skirt length + waist seam and hem. >> Width: half hip (HW) + 20 cm. >> Draw a vertical grain line in red on the centre front (CF) and centre back (CB) 4 cm in from the edge of the fabric, (always begin with this if the model is symmetrical).

>> Indicate the hip height line in red, measuring on the stand from waist to HH line + 5 cm (seam allowance). >> Cut the fabric lengthwise through the middle.

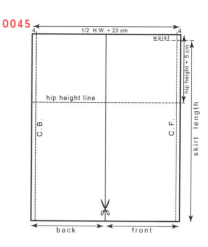

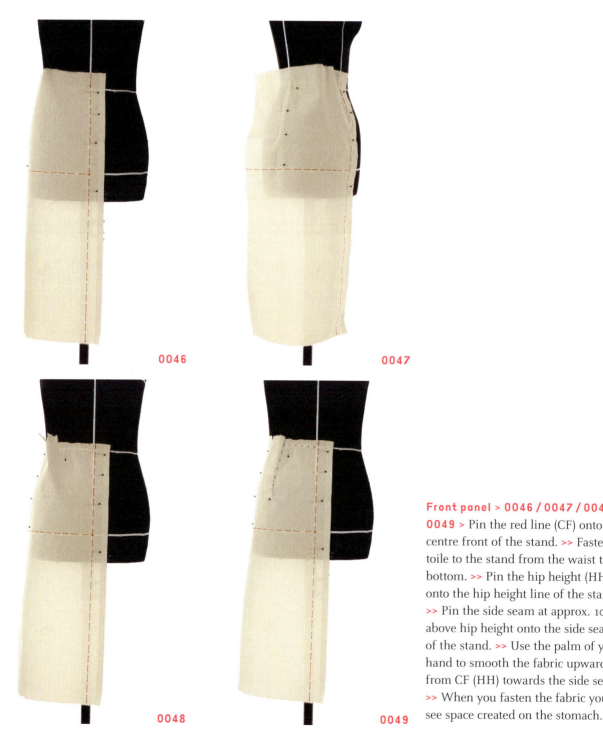

0046

0047

0048

0049

Front panel > 0046 / 0047 / 0048 / 0049 > Pin the red line (CF) onto the centre front of the stand. >> Fasten the toile to the stand from the waist to the bottom. >> Pin the hip height (HH) line onto the hip height line of the stand. >> Pin the side seam at approx. 10 cm above hip height onto the side seam of the stand. >> Use the palm of your hand to smooth the fabric upwards from CF (HH) towards the side seam. >> When you fasten the fabric you will see space created on the stomach.

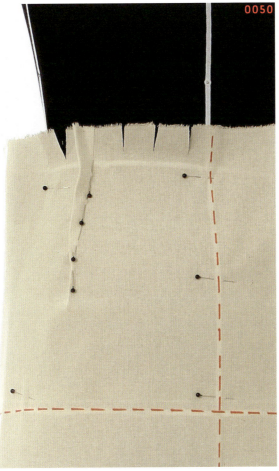

0050

> **0050 >** The space left over in the waist is pinned together into a dart. Pin the two pieces of fabric together (NOT flat). **>>** Cut the seam allowance above the waistline, so that the skirt closes well at the waist. **>>** The position of the dart depends on the form of the body. Make the dart follow the form of the body (that is to say extending outwards a little at the bottom). Do not position the dart too close to the CF, not too close to the side seam.
>> The position of the dart in the waist will be about 7 cm from the side seam.
>> Do not use more than 3.5 cm for the dart - if room is left over then you can better divide the space over two darts.
>> Make the darts no longer than 8-10 cm.

Back panel > 0051 / 0052 > The back panel is draped in the same way. **>>** If the difference between waist and hip is very large, two darts can be placed. **>>** If just one dart is pinned in, then it should lie midway between CB and side seam. In the case of two darts, the waistline is then divided into three equal parts. Follow the form of the body. **>>** Pin the side seams of the front and back panels together. **>>** Mark off the following lines: **>>** CF, CB, waistline, darts on both sides and side seam of the front and back panels. **>>** Remove the toile from the stand and true all the lines, using a ruler or French curve. **>>** Draw from the HH line to the hem. This may be deviated from if you want to make the skirt wider or narrower at the bottom. Take care that the amount added to or removed from the front and back panels is the same (max. 3 cm).

0051

0052

Extra width > 0053 > Extra width is necessary to ensure freedom of movement and because you have draped the toile with the seams on the outside. Decide yourself how much extra width needs to be added, but make sure the same amount is added to or removed from the front and back panels. Note that 0.5 cm extra width per panel becomes 2 cm in the total model.

>> The extra width line can extend to the waist point, but here too extra width can be added. >> If the dress stand is the large size then extra width is not necessary for the final model, as something can always be removed.

0053

0054

Seam allowance > 0054 / 0055 > Draw the seam allowance onto the panels. >> Cut out the panels along these lines. >> Pin the panels together and the darts flat. Check the model on the stand. >> Correct the toile if changes have to be made and mark the corrections.

0055

One-piece gored skirt > **0056** > This skirt is entirely draped. >> Prepare the toile as shown in the example. >> The fabric is ± 1 m long with a width of ± 1.50 m. >> In the middle of the piece of fabric indicate in red the vertical grain line and the horizontal grain line. >> Divide the two halves lengthwise and make diagonal lines between the two lines. This is the true bias. >> One side of the skirt is draped, the other is mirrored.

0056

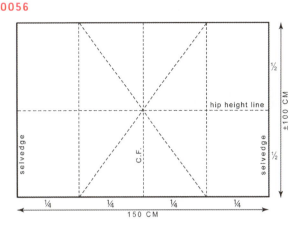

0057

0058

0059

> **0057** > Cut ± 15-20 cm into the fabric at the top at CF. Cut in further if you want more gore. >> Pin this point onto the CF waistline. Make sure there is enough seam allowance at the waist. >> Pin the CF to the stand from the waist down to the bottom. >> Turn away the toile downwards towards the CB so the skirt lies smoothly at the waist and flares at a slant at the bottom. The greater the slant at which the fabric is turned away, the more gore or even flare is created.

> **0058 / 0059** > Cut the fabric horizontally above the waistline and make several incisions as far as the waist band. Continue working in this way as far as CB, drawing the fabric downwards towards CB. >> Cut in above the waistline and make nicks until the toile lies smoothly and then affix. The grain will run more and more diagonally towards the centre back. >> Take care not to stretch the fabric at CB. >> Mark the following lines: >> CF, CB, waistline, side seam and HH line. >> Remove the skirt from the stand. >> Touch up all the lines to make them neat. >> Fold the toile double at CF, mirror the other half.

0060

0061

> **0060** > Mark the seam allowances. Cut out the model.
>> Decide on the length of the skirt, measuring it from the HH line. >> Pin the CB seam flat, leaving ± 25 cm open at the top so the skirt can be tried on.
> **0061** > Check the skirt on the stand.

Flared skirt > 0062 > This skirt is draped from CF to CB. **>>** The amount of fabric required is a skirt length + 1 m. **>>** Prepare the toile as shown in the example.

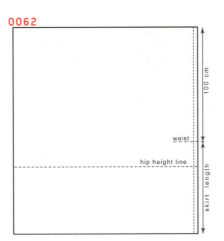

0062

100 cm

waist

hip height line

skirt length

0063

0064

0065

> 0063 > Place pins on the waist and HH lines on the stand immediately above each other at the place where you want the flares to be. In the example shown there are two flares at the front and at the back (more or fewer are possible).

> 0064 / 0065 > Pin the CF and HH lines onto the corresponding lines of the stand. **>>** Make a horizontal nick 1.5 cm above the waistline as far as the first waist pin (position of the first flare). **>>** Smooth the toile flat towards the first pins and fasten the toile to the waistline and HH line at these first pins. **>>** Cut into this 1.5 cm seam allowance as far as the waistband on the stand. Allow the toile to fall away so a flare is created. This flare falls from the nick. Do not pull the fabric - allow it to fall by itself. **>>** Decide on the size of the flare. **>>** Fasten the flare to the HH line next to the previous pin.

>> Repeat this action for each pin as far as CB. **>>** The procedure for each flare is thus: first smooth out and pin as far as the next waist and HH line pin, then make a horizontal nick above the waist, make little cuts towards the waistline, let the flare fall away downwards and attach it to the HH line. **>>** You can make all the flares the same size, or you can decide on the sizes yourself. **>>** Place the fabric smoothly over CB and fasten it with pins.

0066

> **0066** > Mark the following lines: CF, CB, waistline and HH line and add control points to the side seam and at the points where the pins marked the position of the flare. >> Remove the model from the stand. >> True all the lines with a ruler or a French curve. Take care: the waistline does not have to be a smooth, rounded line but can also be a straight or very slightly curved line from nick to nick. If the waistline is accurately marked off then the pleats fall in exactly the same place in the final model. >> Decide on the length of the skirt, measuring it from the HH line. >> Cut 2 cm seam at CB.

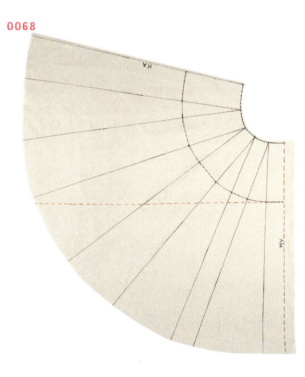

0067   0068

> **0067 / 0068** > Check whether the pleats fall in the right place (they should descend from the nicks).

> Six-piece gored skirt

Six-piece gored skirt > For half a skirt four pieces are prepared. >> Since we are draping only half a skirt, we prepare a half and a whole piece for the front panel and a half and a whole piece for the back panel, making six pieces for a whole skirt.

0069

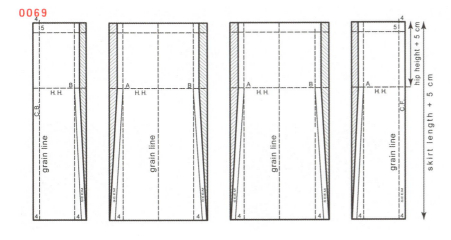

> 0069 > Prepare the toile as shown in the example. Measure the hip of the dress stand and for a six-piece gored skirt divide this distance into six equal parts. This is then the distance A-B.
>> CF and CB become half A-B. >> A-B is placed on the hip height line. It is also possible to place an extra line higher or lower from where the flare is drawn.
>> In this example extra space is at the bottom running from the HH line (the amount depending on the amount of flare). >> Make sure the grain runs straight in the middle of the piece.
>> Draw 2 cm seam on both sides.
>> Number the pieces so as not to get them mixed up. >> Pin the bottom of the skirt flat on the table from HH to hem, pinning the seams flat.

> 0070 / 0071 > Pin CF and CB on the stand. Firmly affix the HH line of all the panels. >> Now pin the grain lines perpendicularly and affix these to the stand. >> In contrast to the standard way of working, drape with the seam on the inside. Make sure the dotted lines stay on top of each other so the same amount of dart is pinned in on both panels. Pin the seam flat.
>> Repeat this procedure for the following pieces. >> Mark all the seams on both the underlying and the top pieces. >> Pin black tape onto the waist to mark the waistline. >> Remove the whole piece from the stand and true all the lines from the HH line to the waist.
>> Mark the seam allowance from the HH line and cut off superfluous fabric.
>> Draw 1 cm seam allowance above the waistline. >> Pin the skirt together and check it on the stand. >> Cut the skirt to the desired length.

0070

0071

Hip piece > 0072 > Prepare the toile as shown in the example.

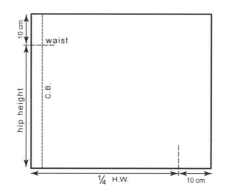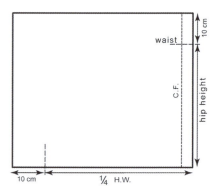

0072

0073

0074

0075

> 0073 / 0074 / 0075 / 0076 > Pin CF onto the stand and smooth down the fabric from CF to the side seam.
>> Cut 1.5 cm seam allowance above the waistline and make nicks as far as the waistband. **>>** Pin CB onto the stand, smooth down the fabric towards the side seam and pin the side seams together. **>>** Indicate the figure line with tape. **>>** Mark the following lines: **>>** CF, CB, side seam and figure line. **>>** You can draw extra width at the side seam. **>>** Cut out the hip piece with seam allowance. **>>** Pin together the hip piece flat and check the model on the stand.

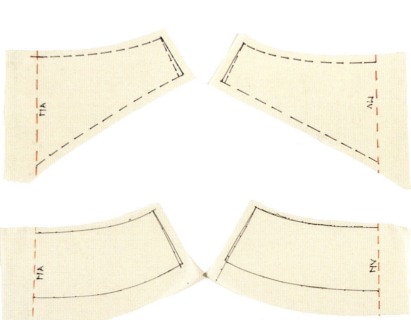

0076

Basic forms:

> Hip piece
> Jupe bombée

Jupe Bombée > For the Jupe Bombée a hip piece is first draped, its length running down to just above the HH line (see p. 52). >> In this example the figure line is horizontal. >> Place the hip piece on the stand, pin the side seam flat. >> Clearly indicate the shape line. >> Take a generous piece of fabric for the skirt part and place CF and CB 4 cm from the fabric's selvedge. >> Gather this long piece of fabric with two threads at the top and one thread at the bottom. The longer the piece of fabric the more volume the skirt has.

0077

0078

> **0077** > Keep the piece raised and pin between the two gather threads to the hip piece on the figure line.
> **0078** > Place the lower gather thread at the bottom of the hip piece. >> Provide a control point on the skirt where the side seam connects to the hip piece.

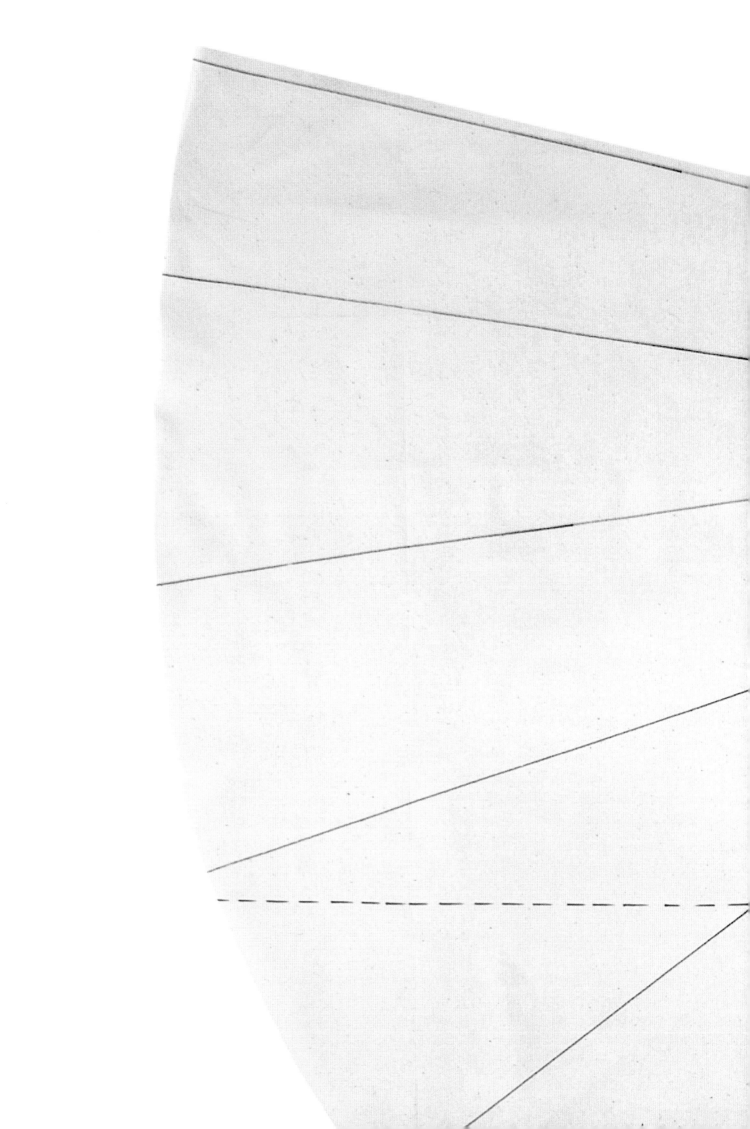

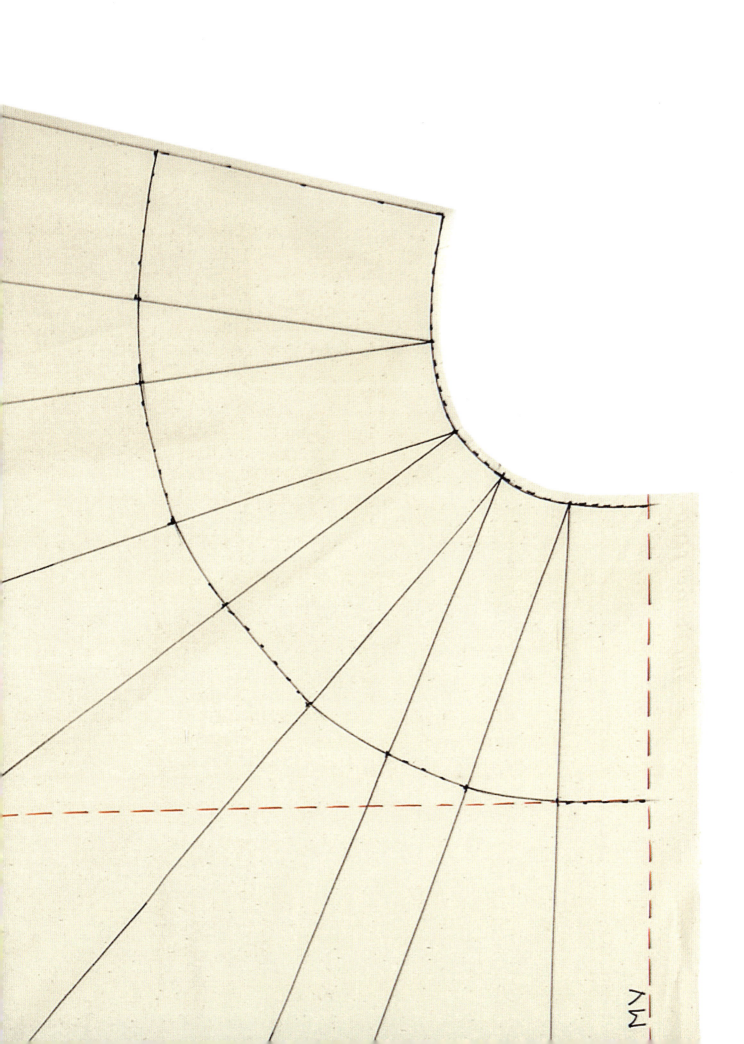

MY

VARIATIONS

Pleats and gathers > **pleats** > **0079** > The space that is otherwise taken up in a dart can also be incorporated in pleats or gathers. >> Extra space can be added from the side seam for more pleats or gathers. >> Mark the side seam. >> Mark the pleats on the waistline on the upper and lower layers of the fabric. >> Mark the waistline with the aid of tape.

Gathers > Pleats pinned into the waist can also be gathered of course. >> Provide control points between which the gathers are to be stitched.

Hip piece with gathers > **0080** > Prepare the toile as shown in the example. Drape the hip piece (see p. 52).

> Straight skirt with high waistline

Variations:
> Pleats and gathers
> Hip piece with gathers

0080

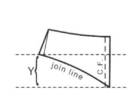

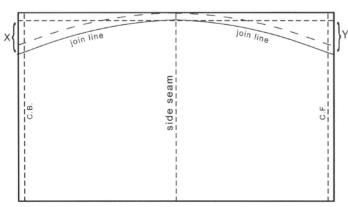

0081 > Take a long piece of fabric and draw the CF and CB 4 cm from the edge of the fabric; the longer the piece of cloth the more gathers (volume). Stitch two gather threads at the top of the piece of fabric. >> Keep the piece raised and pin the skirt between the two gather threads to the hip piece at the figure line indicated (see p. 53).

>> In the model shown here a dropped waistline is indicated with tape.

>> Provide a control point where the skirt part connects to the side seam of the hip piece.

> 0082 > If you decide on a hip piece with a figure line running up or down, then the difference in level is taken up over the whole width so that the grain of the hem remains straight.

0081

0082

Straight skirt with high waistline > 0083 >
Take a piece of fabric the same length as the
desired skirt and with a width of a half HW
+ 20 cm. >> Prepare the toile as shown in the
example and place the CF and CB lines 4 cm
from the edge of the fabric. >> Allow for ± 10
cm extra height above the waist and place the
HH line on the fabric.

> 0084 > Pin the CF and HH lines onto the
corresponding lines of the stand. >> See the
procedure for the straight skirt (p. 44).

0083

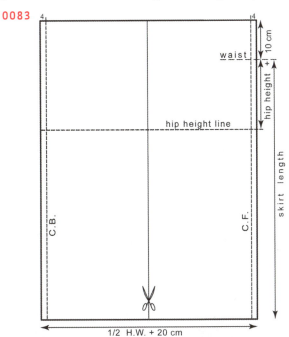

0084

0085

0086

> 0085 / 0086 > Pin the darts and the
side seam through to above the waistline so the skirt remains close to the
body. Take a piece of black tape and
pin it to the top of the skirt to indicate
the desired figure line. >> Mark the
following lines: >> CF, CB, side seam,
darts, waist and figure line. >> Remove
the toile from the stand and true all the
lines. >> Note the desired extra width.
(see p. 41). >> The model can be drawn
in or out a little from the hip to the
bottom, by the same amount on both
panels. >> Mark the seam allowance;
then cut out the panels. >> Pin the panels together flat and check the model
on the stand.

Placing details and figure lines > Details and figure lines can be placed on every design, as we can see in the following example. >> A line is pinned with black tape onto the toile, whereby the panel can be cut to add an extra seam. >> The tape can be placed arbitrarily, according to the design.

0087

0088

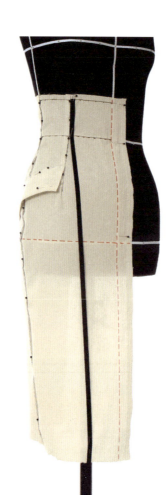

> 0087 > In this example the extra seam nicely follows the line of the dart. >> A piece for a pocket has also been pinned next to the figure line. >> By cutting this detail from toile the size and position of the pocket can be determined according to your own design.
> 0088 > A less well-placed figure line. >> Wrongly applied details or figure lines are detrimental to the model. >> Well-applied details or figure lines can have a corrective effect on the figure and embellish the design.

Wrapped skirt > The example is based on a straight skirt (see p. 44). A wrapped skirt closes right over left when viewed from the dress stand/wearer.
> 0089 > Prepare a whole panel, since this is going to be an asymmetrical model. >> Prepare a half back panel and drape the panel of the straight skirt (see p. 45).

0089

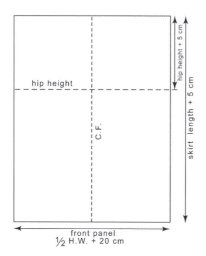

hip height

C.F.

hip height + 5 cm

skirt length + 5 cm

front panel
½ H.W. + 20 cm

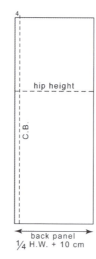

4

hip height

C.B.

back panel
¼ H.W. + 10 cm

0090

0091

> 0090 / 0091 > Pin CF and HH lines to the corresponding lines on the stand. >> Drape the left side; in this case a straight skirt has been decided on, but it can of course also be a different model. >> Determine the size and shape line of the overlap. Here it runs straight, but a figure line can also be indicated on the panel with the aid of black tape. >> Mark the following lines: >> CF, CB, side seam, darts, waist, overlap and figure line. >> True all the lines. >> Mark seam allowances and extra width. >> Cut the skirt to the desired length. >> Pin the panels together flat and check the model on the dress stand. >> If this model is to be made then CB goes against the fold of the fabric and the front panel is mirrored for the right side.

Pleated skirt > Traditionally, a flat pleat is folded right over left as viewed from the dress stand/wearer. >> This pleated skirt consists of twelve pleats. >> Divide the HW + 2 cm extra (more for thicker fabrics) by twelve. >> From CF to CB this makes six pleats = 18 segments, one for the upper pleat and two for the inside pleat. >> For example: HW 94 + 2 cm = 96 : 12 = 8 cm per pleat x 3 = 24 cm + 2 x 4 cm for CF and CB.

> **0092** > Prepare the toile as shown in the example. >> Pin the under pleats flat on the table from the hem to the HH line.

0092

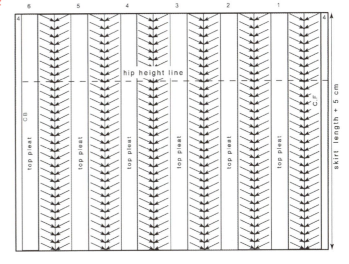

> **0093 / 0094** > Pin CF, CB and HH lines onto the corresponding lines of the stand. >> Affix the HH line firmly with pins. >> Pin the pleat upwards in a straight vertical line. >> In contrast to the standard way of working, drape the seam inwards. >> Make sure the lines of the pleat stay together so that the same amount of dart is pinned off on both panels. >> Pin the seam flat.
> **0095** > Cut away the surplus fabric under the upper layer.

0093

0094

0095

0096

0097

0098

> **0096 / 0097 / 0098** > The lines of the pleats should run perpendicularly following the form of the body. >> Mark the pleats on the upper and under layers. >> Mark the waist with a piece of tape. In this example the waist is somewhat lowered. >> Remove the whole piece from the stand and true all the lines. >> Mark the seam allowance. >> Cut out the pleats with seam allowance. >> Cut the skirt to the desired length.

Pin the panels together flat
and check the model on the stand.

5 BODICES

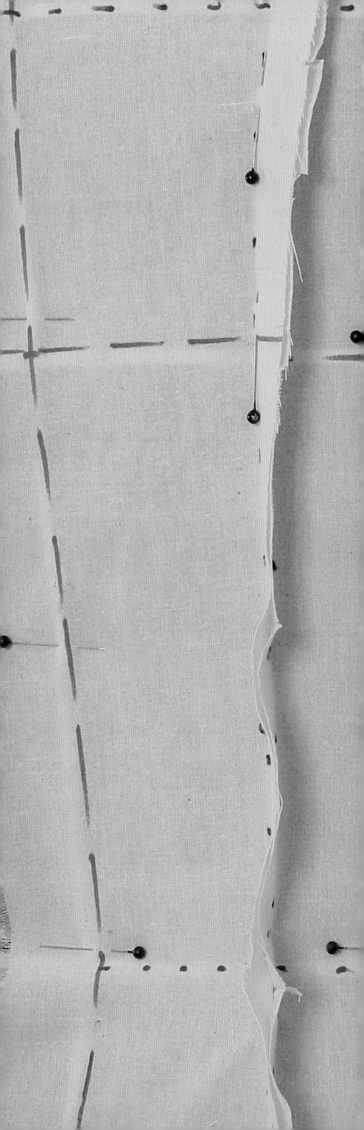

BASIC FORMS

Bodice > 0100 > Begin by taping the dress stand (see p. 34). >> Prepare the toile as shown in the example. Depth: on the front from the shoulder neck point measure one panel length + 5 cm extra height. >> Indicate the following lines on the toile: **Front panel** > CF 4 cm from the edge of the fabric. >> Indicate the BW (Bust) line. Measure on the stand from the shoulder neck point to the BW line + 5 cm extra height. **Back panel** > CB 4 cm from the edge of the fabric. >> Indicate the BW line, which should be at the same height as in the front panel.

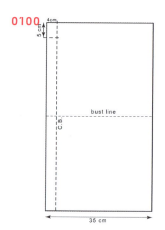
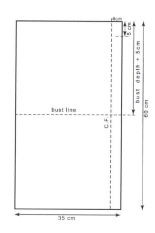

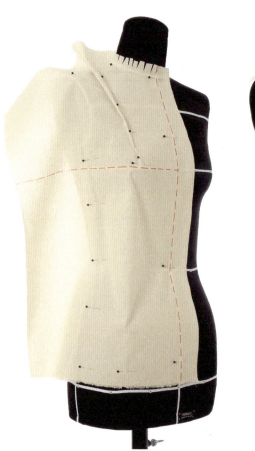

0101

0102

Front panel > 0101 > Pin the CF line onto the CF of the stand. >> Pin the horizontal BW line onto the BW line of the stand. >> Pin the neckline from CF; cut away the toile piece by piece 1 - 1.5 cm above the neckline. >> Cut in the seam allowance as far as the tape. >> Affix the toile to the shoulder. >> Smooth the fabric and pin it from above the BW line towards the shoulder, so that a surplus is created on the shoulder. >> Pin in this surplus to the shoulder dart which lies half way along the shoulder width and runs to ± 2 cm above the bust point. >> If the dress stand has shoulder pieces, you will see surplus fabric beside the arm hole. Cut away some of the fabric, but not too much. >> There is always a small bubble just next to the bust because of the body's curve.

> 0102 > Pin the fabric smoothly down in front of the side seam tape. >> Pin the space created under the bust into a dart in line with the shoulder dart so that it extends down, following the contour of the body, from ± 2 cm under the bust point and approximately in the middle of the front panel.

0103

0104

0105

0106

Back panel > 0103 / 0104 > The back panel is draped in the same way as the front panel. **>>** Make a ± 7 cm dart half way along the shoulder line, corresponding to the dart in the front panel. **>>** Pin the waist dart in line with the shoulder dart approximately in the middle of the back panel following the contour of the body. **>>** Pin together the side seams and shoulder seam of the front and back panels. **>>** Mark the following lines: CF, CB, neckline, waistline, darts on both sides, shoulder seam, arm hole and, if necessary, FCW/BAW line. **>>** Remove both panels from the stand and true all the lines. Always draw the beginning of the arm hole at a right angle to the side seam. **>>** If necessary mark extra width on the side seam and the arm hole.

> 0105 > Cut out the parts of the pattern with seam allowance.

> 0106 > Pin the panels together flat and check the model on the stand. **>>** Cut into the seam allowance if there is still tension on a seam or dart.

Prinsess bodice 1 > 0107 / 0108 > Pin a tape onto the dress stand to indicate the position of the seam. **>>** Prepare the toile as shown in the example. **>>** Mark CF 4 cm from the edge of the fabric. **>>** Mark the BW line. Measure on the stand from shoulder neck point + 5 cm extra height. **>>** Draw a vertical grain line in the centre of each panel.

0107

0108

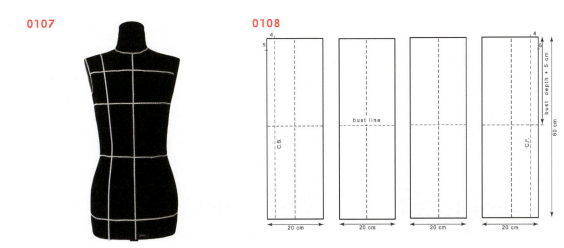

0109

Front panel > 0109 > Pin CF and BW onto the corresponding lines of the stand. **>>** Cut out the neckline and make incisions in the seam allowance so that the fabric lies smoothly across the shoulder. Attach the panel to the

0110

shoulder, waist and hip.
> 0110 > Pin the second panel with BW on the BW line of the stand so that the vertical grain line is kept straight. Even though it looks distorted as it bends with the form of the stand the

0111

line runs straight when seen from a distance of a few metres.
> 0111 > Pin the panels together following the figure line. Cut away the surplus fabric.

0112

0113

Back panel > 0112 / 0113 > The back panel is modelled in the same way. Begin with CB. Make sure that the seam on the shoulder corresponds to the seam of the front panel and that the vertical grain is kept straight. **>>** Pin the shoulder and side seam together. **>>** Mark the following lines: CF, CB, neckline, shoulder seam, arm hole, side seam, panel seams, waistline and, if necessary, FCW/BAW line. **>>** Remove the panels from the stand and true all the lines.
>> Mark extra width as desired on the side seam and the arm hole.

Basic forms: > *Princess bodice 2*

0114

> **0114 / 0115** > Cut out the panels with seam allowances.
>> Pin the panels together flat and check the model on the
stand. >> Cut into the seam allowance if there is still tension
on a seam.

0115

Princess bodice 2 > **0116 / 0117** > Pin a tape onto the dress
stand in order to indicate the position of the figure line.
>> Prepare the toile as shown in the example. >> Draw a
vertical grain line in the centre of each panel.

0116

0117

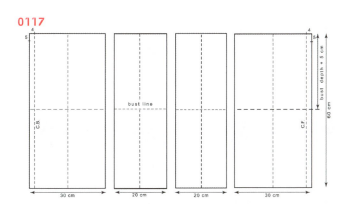

> **0118 / 0119** > Pin CF and BW onto the corresponding lines of the stand. Cut out the neckline and make incisions in the seam allowance so the fabric lies smoothly across the shoulder. >> Pin the fabric to the shoulder, waist and hip. >> Smooth down the fabric from CF to the seam and attach it. >> Cut away surplus fabric, allowing room for seam allowance along the figure line and the arm hole. >> Pin the second panel onto the stand, taking care that the vertical grain line remains straight, and attaching it at the bust waist and hip. Pin the panels together, make nicks in the seam at waist height, affix the side seam in front of the tape. >> Drape the back panel in the same way, beginning with CB. >> Pin together the side seam and the shoulder seam. >> Mark the following lines: CF, CB, neckline, shoulder seam, arm hole, side seam, segment seams on both sides + control points and waistline. >> Remove the panels from the stand and true all the lines. >> If needed, draw extra width on the side seam and the arm hole. >> Cut out the panels with seam allowance. Keep the seams short around the round lines, otherwise they are difficult to handle.

>> Pin the panels together flat and check the model on the stand. >> Cut into the seam allowance if there is still tension on a seam.

0118

0119

Boned bodice (corset) > This model consists of a total of nine panels. In the finished model CF is laid on the fold. >> In this example figure lines are not used on the stand. The seams are formed directly on the desired place on the stand. > **0120** > Prepare five panels as in the example. >> Number the panels.

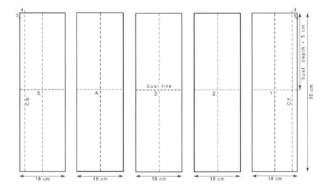

0120

0121

0122

> **0121** > Pin CF and BW to the corresponding lines of the stand. >> Cut out the circular neck and make nicks in the seam allowance so the fabric lies smoothly on the shoulder, and then pin it to the shoulder. > **0122** > Pin the second panel onto the stand, BW line on the BW line of the stand. Make sure the vertical grain line remains straight. This can best be checked by standing a few metres away from the stand.
>> Pin the seams together across the bust point. The seam runs from half-way along the shoulder across the bust point and follows the form of the body.
>> Cut away surplus fabric.

0123

0124

0125

> **0123** > Pin the third panel onto the stand, again with a straight grain line, the BW line on the BW line of the stand. Pin the seams together. The seam runs straight up from the waist and follows the form of the body below the waist. > **0124** > Pin the fourth panel onto the stand, BW line on the BW line of the stand and pin the seams together. Take care that the grain line is vertical. The seam runs straight up from the waist and follows the form of the body under the waist. > **0125** > Pin

the fifth panel onto the stand, CB on CB and BW line on the corresponding lines of the stand. Cut out the circular neck and make nicks in the seam allowance.
>> Pin the last seam which connects with the seam of the front panel.
>> Check whether the seams have been well positioned and the panels are regularly divided so as to form a nice hour-glass shape. >> Mark the following lines: CF, CB, neckline, shoulder seam, arm hole, segment seams, waist-

line and, if necessary, BAW/FCW line.
>> Remove the panels from the stand and true all the lines.

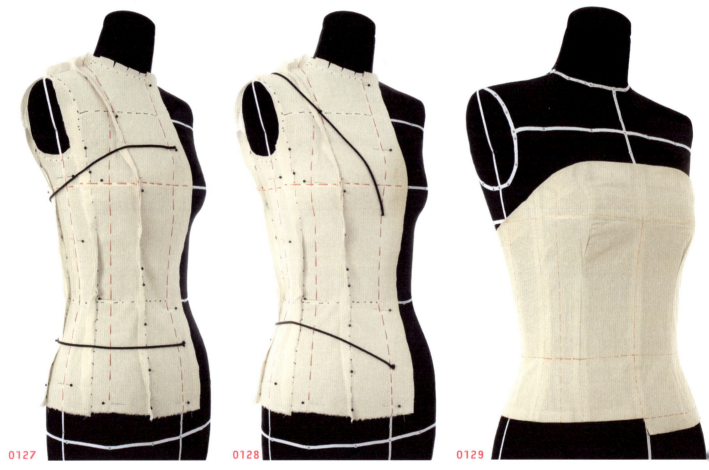

> **0126** > Mark, if desired, extra width in seam 2 and 3 (side panel) and the arm hole. >> Cut out the panels with seam allowance. >> Pin the panels together flat and check the model on the stand.

0127

0128

0129

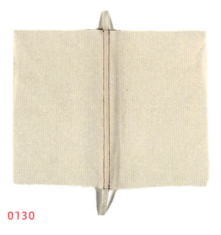

0130

> **0127 / 0128 / 0129** > A figure line can now be applied to the model with the aid of black tape. > **0130** > With a strapless model the boning is stitched exactly behind the folded open seam.

Straight bodice > **0131** > Prepare the toile as shown in the example. In this example an extra vertical grain line is placed in the panel so you can clearly see how the grain runs in the panel. You can indicate several grain lines on the toile as you see fit.

0131

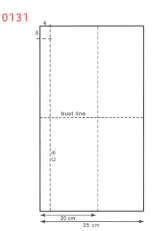
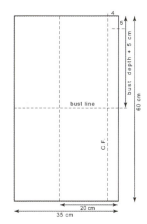

0132

0133

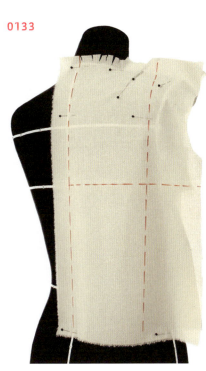

0134

0135

> **0132** > Pin CF and BW lines onto the corresponding lines on the stand.
>> Cut out the circular neckline and make nicks in the seam allowance.
>> Attach the fabric to the shoulder and smooth it flat towards the arm hole.
>> Make a small bust dart towards the side seam so that the panel hangs straight. >> Attach the side seam in front of the tape. > **0133** > Pin CB and BW lines onto the corresponding lines on the stand. >> Cut out the circular neckline and make nicks in the seam allowance. >> Attach the toile with straight grain next to the shoulder blade. >> Pin a shoulder dart half way along the shoulder.

> **0134 / 0135** > Pin the shoulder and side seam downwards in a straight line. >> Mark the following lines: CF, CB, neckline, shoulder seam, arm hole, side seam and darts. >> Remove the panels from the stand and true all the lines. >> Mark, if desired, extra width on the side seam and the arm hole. >> Cut out the panels with seam allowance. > **0136** > Pin the panels together flat and check the model on the stand.

0136

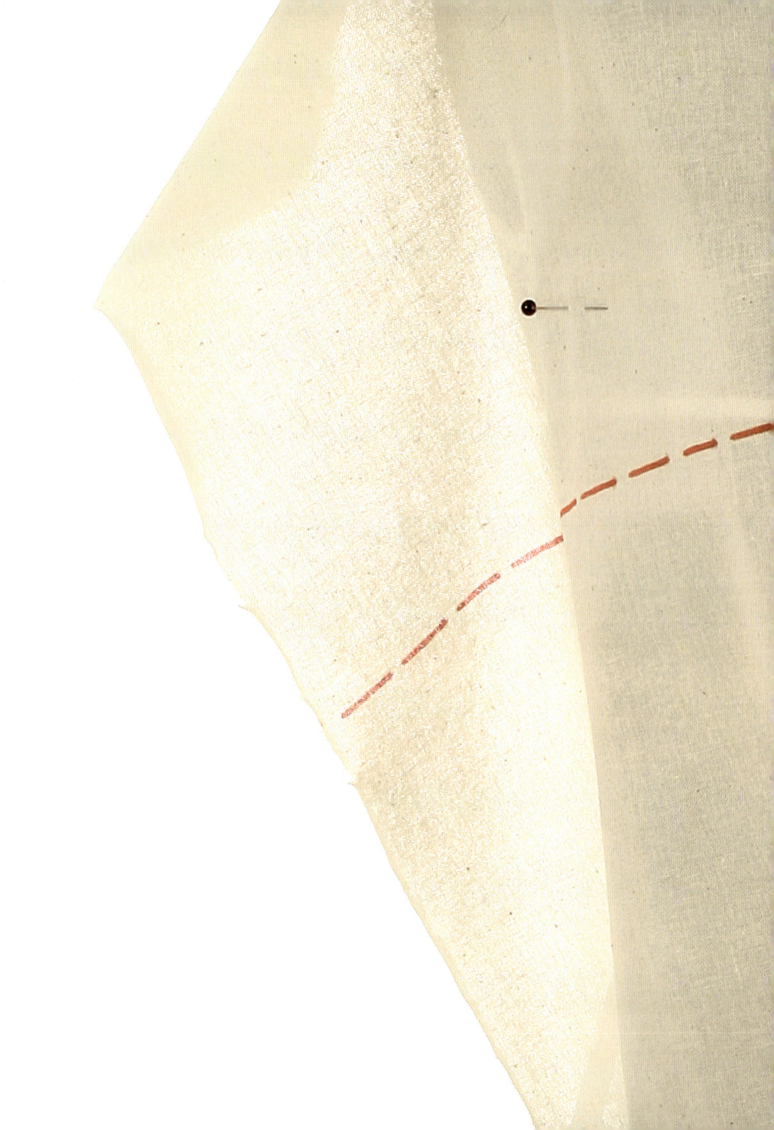

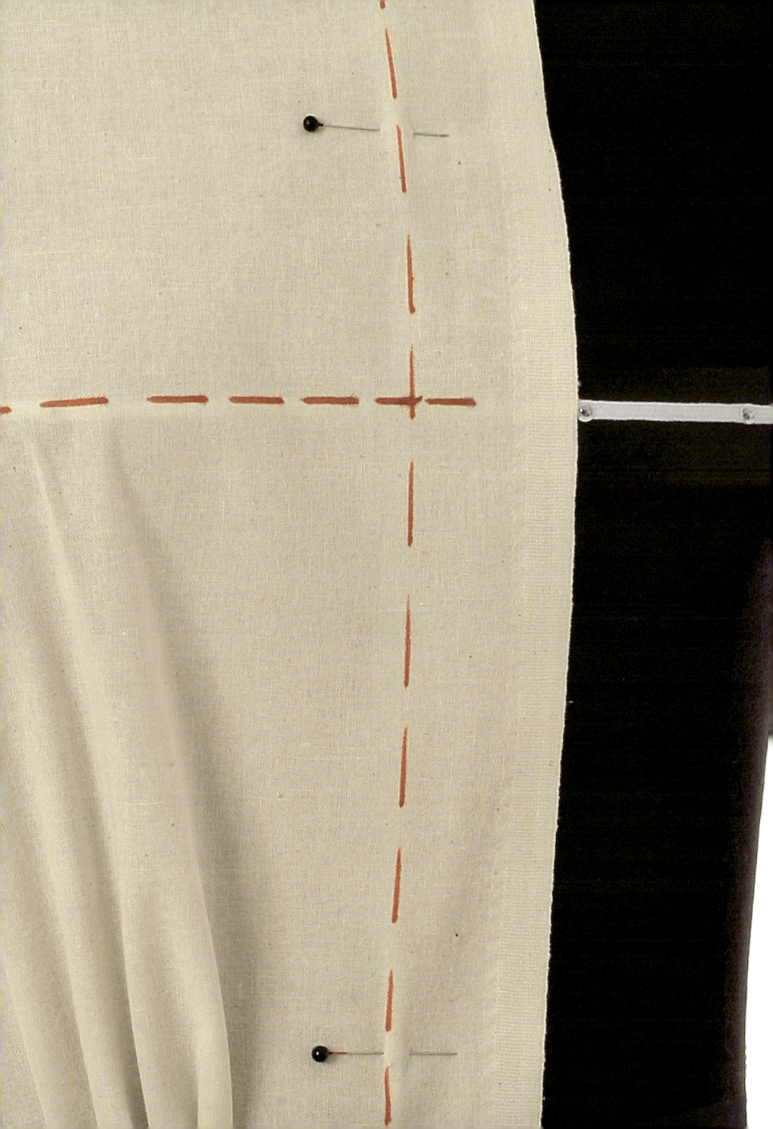

VARIATIONS

Dart variations > You can alter the cut by moving darts to another position or making more space in a different way. As the following examples show, the darts in the front panel can be made to run in several directions.

> 0137 > Prepare a front panel according to the example. **> 0138 >** Pin CF and BW to the corresponding lines on the stand.

0137

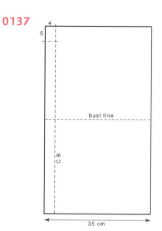
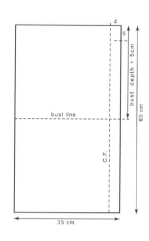

0138

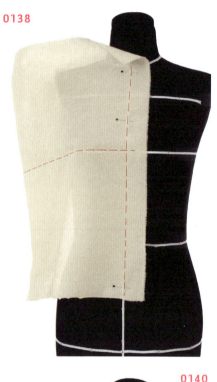

0139

0140

0141

> 0139 > The dart runs from the bust point to the neckline, so that the panel falls straight at the waist. **> 0140 >** The dart runs smoothly from the bust point to CF. CF turns the fabric past the CF on the stand and the dart is pinned horizontally onto the BW line, so that the panel falls straight at the waist. **> 0141 >** The dart is turned towards the waist and gathered in. **>>** If the white waist band on the stand is no longer visible you can attach a black tape across the gathers so the waistline can be marked accordingly.

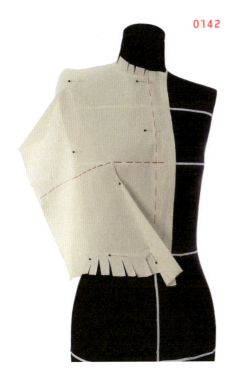

0142

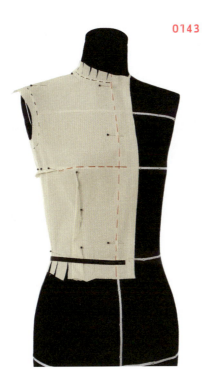

0143

> **0142 >** The dart runs from the bust point diagonally to CF waistline.
> **0143 >** The dart runs from the bust point to the waist and the side seam, so the space is now taken up by darts in two places.

Figure line cut 1 > Here the figure line passes over the BW line. The seam can also have a different form. Make sure the line runs more or less across the bust point, since then the dart can be incorporated into the seam.

0144

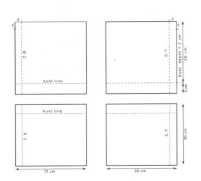

> **0144 >** Prepare the toile as shown in the example. **Upper panel > 0145 >** Pin CF and BW to the corresponding lines on the stand. **>>** The BW line will sink a little as it goes past the bust point since the toile is laid smoothly onto the shoulder. **>>** Cut out the circular neckline and make nicks in the seam allowance. **>>** Pin shoulder and side seam.

0145

Lower panel > 0146 > Pin CF on the CF of the stand. **>>** Pin the seam horizontally across the BW line. The dart is incorporated into this. **>>** Smooth down the toile towards the side seam. **>>** Cut away surplus fabric under the waist line and make nicks in the seam allowance so the waist can be laid smoothly. **>>** The rear panel is draped in the same way as the front panel, with the addition of a dart at the shoulder. **>>** Pin the shoulder seam and side seam together. **>>** Mark the following lines: CF, CB, neckline, shoulder seam, shoulder dart, arm hole, side seam, segment seam and waistline. **>>** Remove the panels from the stand and true all the lines. **>>** Mark, if desired, extra width on the side seam and the arm hole. **>>** Cut out the panels with seam allowance. **>>** Pin the panels together flat and check the model on the stand.

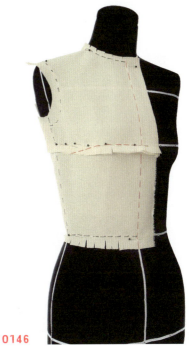

0146

Figure line cut 2 asymmetrical > 0147 >

Use a tape to indicate a figure line on the stand. The dart is best incorporated when the line runs more or less across the bust point.

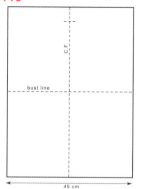
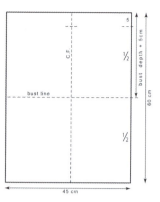

0147

> 0148 > Prepare the toile as shown in the example. > 0149 > For an asymmetrical model a whole front panel is prepared. >> Pin CF and BW onto the corresponding lines on the stand.
>> Cut out the neckline and make nicks in the seam allowance.
>> Indicate the diagonal figure line of the stand on the toile. >> Cut out the uppermost part with seam allowance and fix the toile along the figure line with pins. >> If the toile lies flat on the shoulder the BW line will sink a little to the side from the bust point.

> 0150 > Pin CF and BW of the second panel onto the corresponding lines on the stand. >> Pin the diagonal seams together across the figure line and cut away surplus fabric.

> 0151 > Make a dart in the right-hand panel of the bust point to CF, the same direction as the seam. >> Cut away surplus fabric under the waistline and make nicks in the seam allowance so that the toile can be laid flat.
>> Mark the following lines: CF, CB, neckline, shoulder seams, arm hole, side seam, segment seam and dart.
>> Remove the panels from the stand and true all the lines.

> 0152 > Mark, if desired, extra width on the side seam and the arm hole. Cut out the panels with seam allowance. >> Pin the panels together flat and check the model on the stand.

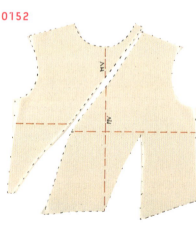

0153

0154

0155

Arm hole variations > 0153 / 0154 > If no sleeve is placed in the panel then an arm hole can have virtually any desired form. >> Place a front and back panel on the stand and pin the seams together flat. Use black tape to indicate the form of the arm hole.

Neckline variations > 0155 > Place a front and back panel on the stand and pin the seams together flat. A neckline can have almost any desired shape. >> Use black tape to indicate the form of the neckline.

Shoulder yoke > 0156 / 0157 / 0158 > Place a front and back panel on the stand and pin the seams together flat. >> Use black tape to indicate the shape of the shoulder yoke on the front and/or back panel. >> The shoulder yoke can have any desired form.

0158

0156

0157

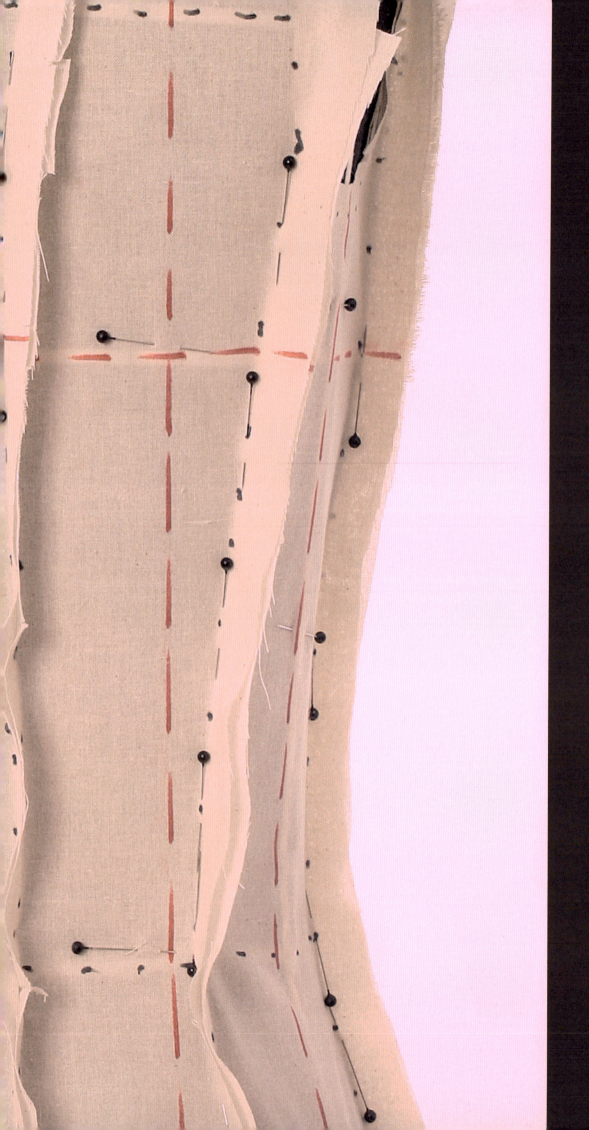

6 DRESSES

Basic forms:
80 > *Fitted dress*
82 > *Straight dress*
83 > *Flared dress*

Variations:
87 > *Dress with waist seam*
88 > *Dress with low waist*
89 > *Dress with high waist*

BASIC FORMS

Fitted dress > **0159** > Prepare the toile as shown in the example. Height: on the front from the shoulder neck point measure 1 x length of dress + 5 cm extra height. >> Indicate the following lines on the toile:

Front panel > CF 4 cm from the edge of the fabric. >> Indicate the BW (bust) and HH (hip height) lines. Measure on the stand from the shoulder neck point to the BW and HH lines + 5 cm extra height.

Back panel > CB 4 cm from the edge of the fabric. >> Indicate the BW and HH lines, which should be at the same height as in the front panel.

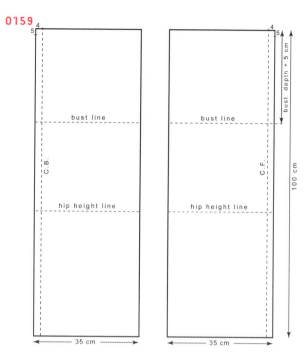

0159

Front panel > **0160** > Pin CF, BW and HH lines onto the corresponding lines of the stand. >> Cut out the neckline piece by piece and make nicks in the seam allowance. >> Pin the shoulder dart, which lies halfway along the shoulder width and runs to ± 2 cm above the bust point. >> If the dress stand has shoulder pieces, you will see surplus fabric beside the arm hole. Cut away some of the fabric, but not too much. >> There is always a small bubble just next to the bust because of the body's curve.

> **0161** > Pin the waist dart in line with the shoulder dart, following the contour of the body, starting ± 2 cm under the bust point and approximately in the middle of the front panel.

0160

0161

Back panel > 0162 > Pin CB, BW and HH lines onto the corresponding lines of the stand. **>>** The back panel is draped in the same way as the front panel. **>>** Make a ± 7 cm shoulder dart half way along the shoulder line, corresponding to the dart in the front panel. **>>** Pin the waist dart in line with the shoulder dart so that it runs approximately in the middle of the back panel. **>>** Pin the shoulder and side seams together. **>>** Mark the following lines: CF, CB, neckline, waistline, darts, shoulder seam, side seam, arm hole and, if necessary, FCW/BAW line. **>>** Remove the panels from the stand and true all the lines. Always draw the beginning of the arm hole at a right angle to the side seam.

> 0163 > If necessary mark extra width on the side seam and the arm hole (see p. 41). **>>** Cut out the panels with seam allowance.

> 0164 > Pin the panels together flat and check the model on the stand. **>>** Cut into the seam allowance if there is still tension on a seam or dart. **>>** Cut the model to the desired length.

0162

0163

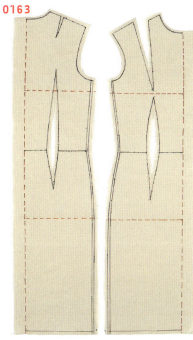

0164

Straight dress > Prepare the toile (see previous model p. 80).

Front panel > 0165 > Pin CF, BW and HH lines onto the corresponding lines of the stand. Make sure that the BW and HH lines run horizontally. **>>** Pin the fabric smoothly across the shoulder. **> 0166 >** If the stand has shoulders, cut out the arm hole. **>>** Pin a small bust dart from the side seam to the bust point so the BW and HH lines continue to run horizontally. **>>** Pin the side seam down in a straight line.

0165

0166

0167

0168

Back panel > 0167 > Pin CB, BW and HH lines onto the corresponding lines of the stand. **>>** Cut out the neckline and make incisions in the seam allowance. **>>** Cut out the arm hole. **>>** Pin the shoulder and side seams together.
> 0168 > Mark the following lines: CF, CB, neckline, shoulder seam, arm hole, side seam and the dart. **>>** Remove the panels from the stand and true all the lines.

> **0169** > Mark extra width as desired on the side seam and the arm hole.
>> Cut out the panels with seam allowances. > **0170** > Pin the panels together flat and check the model on the stand.
>> Cut the dress to the desired length.

0169

0170

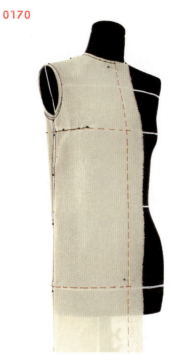

Flared dress > **0171** > Prepare the toile as shown in the example. **Front panel** > **0172** > Pin CF, BW and HH line onto the corresponding lines of the stand. >> Cut out the neckline and make nicks in the seam allowance. >> Fix the shoulder. >> Place a bust dart towards the side seam. >> If the stand has shoulders a piece of the arm hole now has to be cut away. >> Give some extra space in the panel. Now the BW and HH lines drop towards the side seam.

0172

0171

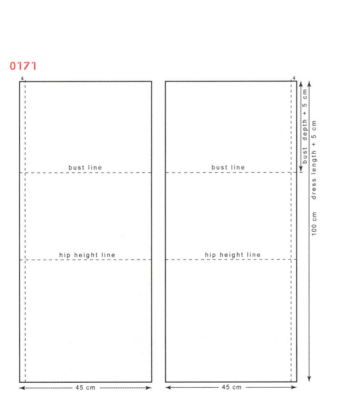

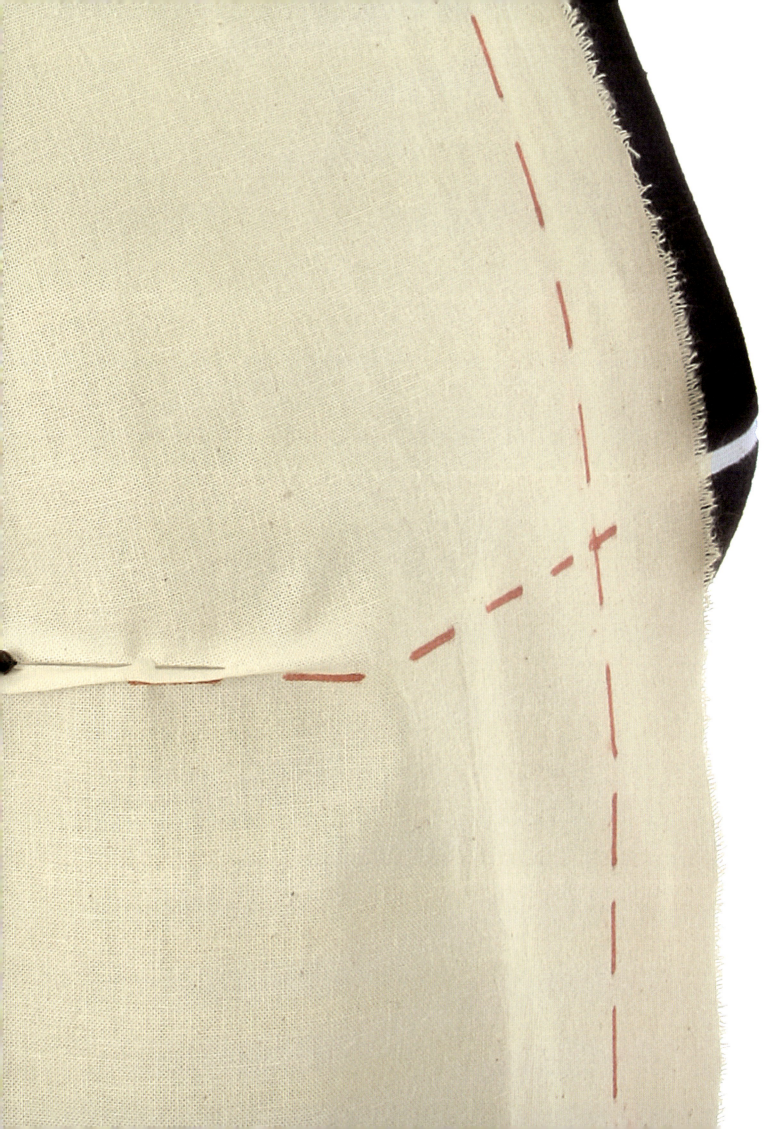

0173

Back panel > Pin CB, BW and HH lines onto the corresponding lines of the stand. >> Cut out the neckline and make nicks in the seam allowance. >> Add some extra space in the panel to eliminate the need for a dart. Smooth down the shoulder. >> Cut out the arm hole. >> Pin shoulder seam and side seam together. >> Mark the following lines: CF, CB, neckline, arm hole, side seam and the dart. >> Remove the whole piece from the stand and true the lines.

> **0173** > Mark extra width as desired on the side seam and the arm hole. >> Cut out the panels with seam allowance.

> **0174** > Pin the panels together flat and check the model on the stand. >> Cut the dress to the desired length.

0174

VARIATIONS

Dress with waist seam > Bodices and skirts can be put together to form a dress with waist seam. >> Many variations are thus possible. >> Prepare the toile for a basic bodice (see p. 64).

> **0175** > Here the shoulder dart has been moved to CF. >> Mark the following lines: CF, CB, neckline, shoulder seam, arm hole, side seam and the darts. >> Remove the whole piece from the stand and true the lines. >> Pin the panels together flat and check the model on the stand.

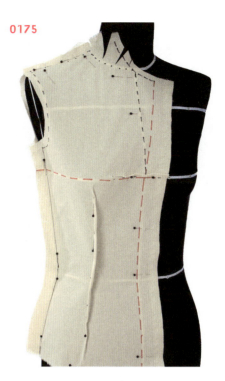

0175

0176

0177

0178

> **0176** > Prepare the toile for a straight skirt (see p. 44). >> Pin CF and HH line onto the corresponding lines of the stand. >> Instead of a dart in the waist, pleats are made with extra fabric added from the side seam. >> Pin the skirt seam, tapering slightly inwards

towards the hem (tube skirt).

> **0177** > Place a tape in the waist where the waist seam is to come. >> Mark the following lines: CF, CB, waist line and the pleats on the upper and lower layers. >> Remove the whole toile from the stand and true the lines.

Mark extra width as desired on the side seam and the arm hole. >> Cut out the panels with seam allowance.

> **0178** > Pin the panels together flat and check the model on the stand. >> Cut the dress to the desired length.

Dress with low waist > **Bodice** > Prepare the toile for a bodice (see p. 64). >> Ensure that the panel is long enough. > **0179** > Pin the seams of the desired model flat and check it on the stand. >> Place a black tape to indicate the figure line at the point where the skirt is to be attached to the panel. >> Here the shape is straight, but it can just as easily take another form.

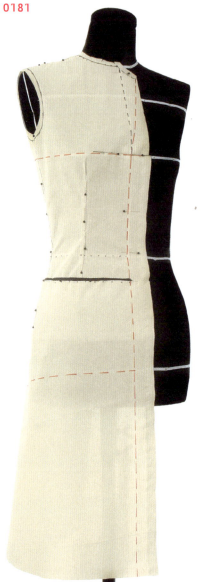

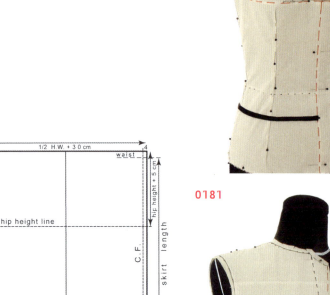

0180

Skirt > **0180** > Any type of skirt can be attached to a bodice >> Here a slightly flared skirt has been chosen. >> Prepare the toile according to the example. > **0181** > Pin CF and HH line onto the corresponding lines of the stand. >> Turn the toile down a little towards the side seam for the flare. The HH line will drop a little at the side seam. >> The back panel is draped in the same way. >> Pin the side seams together. >> Mark the following lines: CF, CB, side seam, join line and HH line. >> Remove the whole piece from the stand and true the lines. >> Mark extra width as desired on the side seam and the arm hole. >> Cut out the panels with seam allowance. >> Pin the panels together flat and check the model on the stand. >> Cut the dress to the desired length.

Variations:

> Dress with low waist

> Dress with high waist

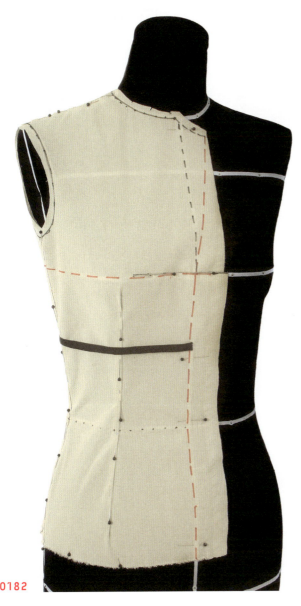

0182

0183

Dress with high waist > Bodice > 0182 >
Here the bodice from the previous model is used. >> Pin the desired model together flat and check it on the stand. >> Place a black tape to indicate the figure line at the point where the skirt is to be attached to the panel.

> **0183** > Any type of skirt can be attached to a bodice. Here a fitted skirt with a waist dart has been chosen.Prepare the toile for a fitted skirt with 20 cm extra above the waist.
>> Pin CF and HH line onto the corresponding lines of the stand. >> The HH line runs horizontally towards the side seam. >> Pin the waist dart in line with the waist dart of the upper panel. >> The back panel is draped in the same way as the front panel. >> Pin the side seam together. >> Mark the following lines: CF, CB, side seam, join line and the darts.
>> Remove the whole piece from the stand and true all the lines. >> Mark extra width as desired on the side seam and the arm hole. >> Cut out the panels with seam allowance.

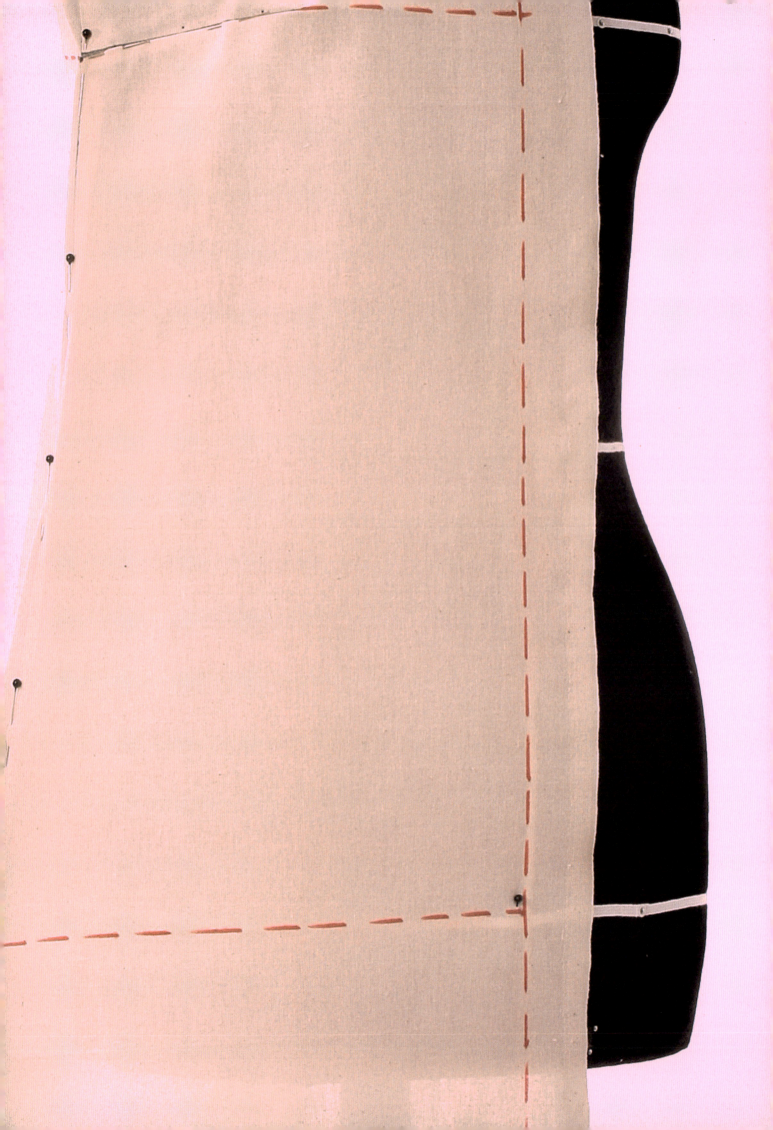

7 SLEEVES

BASIC FORMS

One-piece sleeve > Straight sleeve > For draping sleeves the arm is used (see pp. 38/39).

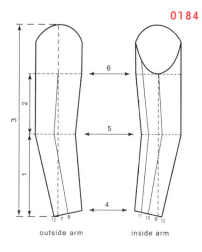

0184

outside arm   inside arm

> 0184 > Outer arm > 1 Lower arm **>>** 2 Upper arm **>>** 3 Arm length **>>** 4 Wrist line **>>** 5 Elbow line **>>** 6 Upper arm line **>>** 7 Grain line **>>** 8 Upper sleeve seam **>>** 12 Back sleeve seam

Inner arm > 9 Grain line **>>** 10 Inner sleeve seam **>>** 11 Front sleeve seam **>>** 12 Back sleeve seam

>> Before the sleeve can be draped, a front and back panel have to be placed on the stand, with a good arm hole (in other words, an arm hole that suits the type of sleeve that is going to be draped). **>>** A fitted sleeve requires a smaller arm hole than with a wider sleeve. **>>** The straight sleeve, two-piece sleeve and the raglan sleeve usually need a slightly roomier arm hole. **>>** If shoulder padding is used then place this onto the stand before draping the panel and sleeve (see p. 37). **>>** Drape the front and back panels as desired and deepen the arm hole.

0185

0186

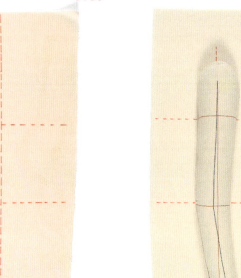

> 0185 / 0186 > Prepare the toile as follows: **>>** Take a piece of fabric 45 cm wide and the length of the sleeve + 10 cm. **>>** Place a vertical grain line in the middle of the fabric (7). **>>** Place a horizontal line 2 cm from the bottom (wrist line 4). **>>** Measure the distance from the wrist line to the elbow on the arm and trace this line parallel to the wrist line on the toile (5). **>>** Measure the distance from the elbow on the arm to the upper arm and trace this line as well (6).

0187

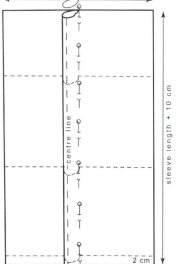

total 45 cm

centre line

sleeve length + 10 cm

2 cm

> 0187 > In the middle of the piece of fabric pin a pleat measuring a total of 4-5 cm for the required extra width, so that the raised part is then 2-2.5 cm.

> 0188 > Pin the fold and grain line to the grain line of the outside arm (7 red line).

0188

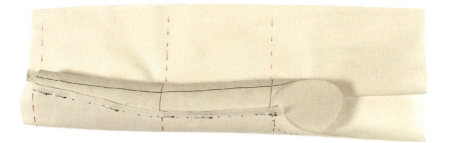

0189

0190

> **0189** > Turn the arm around so that the inner arm is on top and pin the toile to the inner arm seam (10). >> Cut away surplus fabric.

> **0190** > Fold the other side towards the inner arm seam and pin the fabric together. >> Mark the seam and the lower arm hole.

0191

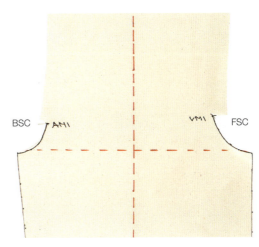

BSC   AMI   VMI   FSC

> **0191** > Indicate the front sleeve cross mark (FSC) which lies 9.5 cm from the inner sleeve seam. >> Indicate the back sleeve cross mark (BSC) which lies 7.5 cm from the lower sleeve seam. >> Remove the sleeve from the arm and true the lines.

> **0192** > Pin the draped panel flat onto the stand. >> Hang the arm on the stand, taking care that the grain line points a little to the front (red line). >> Indicate the FSC in the arm hole on the front panel; this lies 9.5 cm from the side seam. >> Indicate the BSC in the arm hole on the front panel; this lies 7.5 cm from the side seam.

0191

0192

> **0193** > Pin together the sleeve flat. A simple way to do this is to insert a ruler and to use this as a backing to pin against.

0193

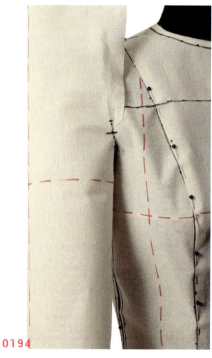

0194

0195

0196

> **0194 / 0195** > Place the FSC and BSC of the sleeve on the FSC and BSC of the panel. >> Make nicks in the sleeve at these points, exactly as far as the pin!

> **0196** > Fold the upper piece of the sleeve across the arm hole and pin the head to the panel. >> Divide the space between the pins as equally as possible. >> Cut away surplus fabric. >> The grain line of the sleeve does not have to connect with the shoulder seam; it is only an aid in hanging the grain of the sleeve properly.

> **0197 / 0198** > With a high head there is space left in the head, but this can be incorporated in the diagonal grain when putting in the sleeve.

0197

0198

> **0199** > Pin the seam allowance inwards and divide the space equally. >> If there is too much space in the head then pin in more seam allowance. >> Mark the head and put control points on panel and sleeve. >> Decide on the length of the sleeve and mark accordingly. >> Remove the sleeve from the stand and true the head and hem.

Sleeve with flat head > With a flat head sleeve the arm does not hang alongside the body but is kept in a raised position (by means of a tape, for example). Determine the position of the arm as you see fit. The higher the position of the arm the less cap space the sleeve will have. >> The procedure for the flat head sleeve is the same as that for the previous sleeve.

0200

0201

> **0200** > The position of the arm makes the head flatter and less space is created in the head. >> Pin the seam inwards. >> Mark the head and put control points on panel and sleeve. >> Decide on the length of the sleeve and mark accordingly. >> Remove the sleeve from the stand and true the head and hem.

> **0201** > The difference between the high and flat sleeve head is clearly visible in this example.

Fitted sleeve > This sleeve is draped on the basis of the one-piece sleeve. It has the same head as the one-piece sleeve (see p. 92) but has more shape between the elbow and the wrist. >> Follow the same procedure as for the straight sleeve.

0202

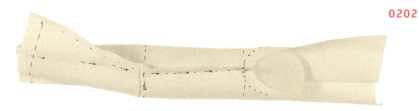

> **0202** > Pin the lower sleeve from the elbow smoothly around the lower arm onto the inner sleeve seam (10). >> A small dart is now created on the elbow line. >> Cut away surplus fabric.

0203

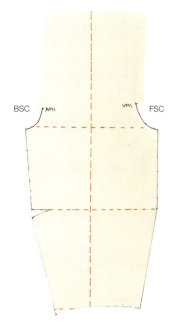

0204

> **0203 / 0204 >** Fold the other side towards the inner arm seam and pin the fabric together. **>>** Cut away surplus fabric. **>>** Mark the seam, dart, wrist and lower arm hole. **>>** Indicate the FSC which lies 9.5 cm from the inner sleeve seam. **>>** Indicate the BSC which lies 7.5 cm from the inner sleeve seam. **>>** Remove the sleeve from the arm and true all the lines. **>>** Pin the sleeve together flat and pin the sleeve into the panel. The rest of the procedure is the same as for the straight sleeve.

Two-piece sleeve > 0205 > Prepare two pieces of toile - a broad strip for the outer arm and a narrower one for the inner arm. **>>** Prepare the toile as follows:

0205

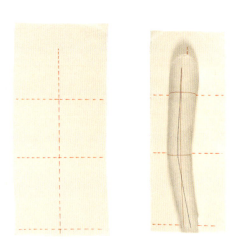

Outer arm > Take a piece of fabric sleeve length + 10 cm long and 30 cm wide. **>>** Place a horizontal line 2 cm from the bottom (wrist line 4). **>>** From this line measure the distance to the elbow on the arm and trace this line parallel to the wrist line on the toile (5). **>>** Measure the distance from the elbow on the arm to the upper arm line and trace this line as well (6). **Inner arm >** Take a second piece of fabric the length of the sleeve + 10 cm and 25 cm wide. **>>** Place a vertical grain line in the middle of the piece and the same horizontal lines as on the outer arm.

> **0206 / 0207 >** In the middle of both pieces pin a pleat measuring a total of 2-3 cm for the required extra width, so that the raised part is then 1-1.5 cm.

0206   **0207**

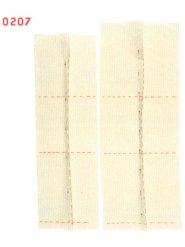

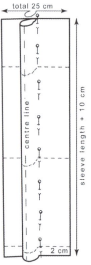

Basic forms:

> Two-piece sleeve
> Raglan

0208

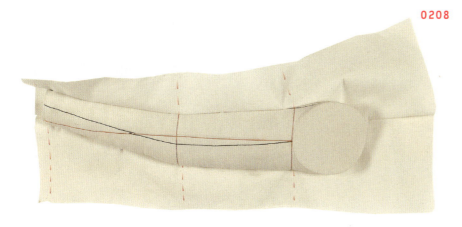

> **0208** > On the outer arm pin the fold onto the grain line of the arm (7). >> Pin the fabric as far as the back sleeve seam (12). >> Pin the other side as far as the front sleeve seam of the inner arm (11). >> Cut away surplus fabric.

0209

> **0209** > Pin the second piece onto the inner arm with the pleat onto the grain line and fasten the fabric as far as the front and back sleeve seam. >> Pin these seams together and cut away surplus fabric. >> Mark the arm hole and the seams on the sleeve.
>> Indicate FSC 9.5 cm and BSC 7.5 cm on the sleeve. >> Remove the sleeve from the arm and unfasten the extra width pleat. >> True the lines. >> Pin the sleeve together flat.

> **0210 / 0211 / 0212** > Pin the FSC and BSC of the sleeve onto the FSC and BSC of the panel. >> Make nicks in the sleeve at these points. >> Drape the head of the sleeve and decide on the length. >> Mark head and hem, put control marks on the sleeve head and front and back panels. >> Remove the sleeve from the stand and true all lines.

0210

0211

0212

Raglan sleeve > **0213** > Prepare the toile as shown in the example. Sleeve length + 20 cm and a width of 45 cm. **>>** A one-piece or two-piece sleeve can be used as a raglan sleeve. **>>** Drape a sleeve on the arm as desired. **>>** Cut into the sleeve at FSC and BSC.

0213

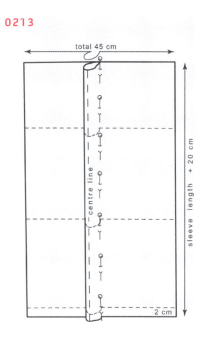

> **0214** > Use tape to indicate the raglan shape on the front and back panels.

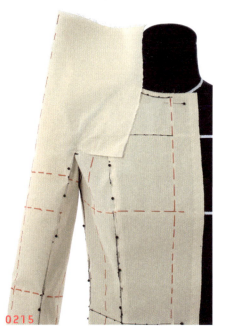

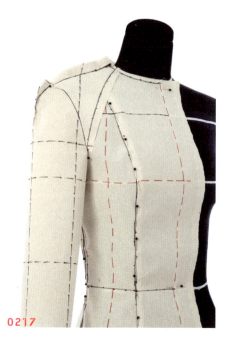

0217

> **0215** > Pin the sleeve into the lower arm hole from FSC to BSC. **>>** Make nicks in the sleeve at these points. **>>** Lay the shoulder part of the sleeve from FSC to BSC smoothly across the panel. > **0216** > Pin the shoulder seam and taper it to a point, ending at a dart in the sleeve head. **>>** Decide on the length of the sleeve. **>>** Cut away surplus fabric. **>>** Mark the following lines: neckline, shoulder seam, raglan shape and the hem.

> **0217** > Remove the sleeve from the panel and true all the sleeve and panel lines. **>>** Cut out the sleeve and the panel with seam allowance, pin the seams flat onto each other and check the model on the stand.

0218

0219

0220

> 0218 / 0219 / 0220 > The raglan sleeve can have a variety of shapes. >> In the example the raglan shape runs to the neck, but it can also run to the shoulder. If the raglan runs through to CF or CB then more fabric width is needed for draping the sleeve.

Kimono sleeve > 0221 > Prepare the toile as shown in the example. > 0222 > Hang the arm in the desired position on the stand, in line with the shoulder seam.

0221

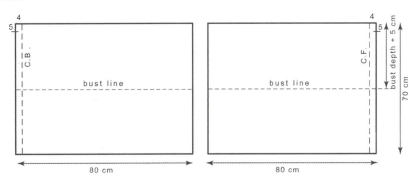

0222

> 0223 > Pin the CF and BW lines onto the corresponding lines of the stand.
> 0224 > Pin the CB and BW lines onto the corresponding lines of the stand.
>> Cut out the neckline and make nicks in the seam allowance. >> Lay the toile smoothly across the shoulder and pin the shoulder and upper arm seam.

0223   0224

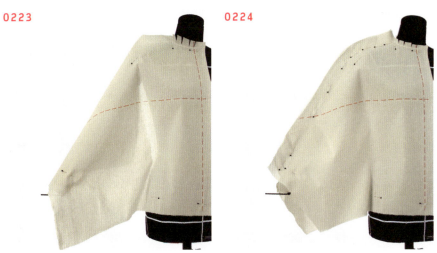

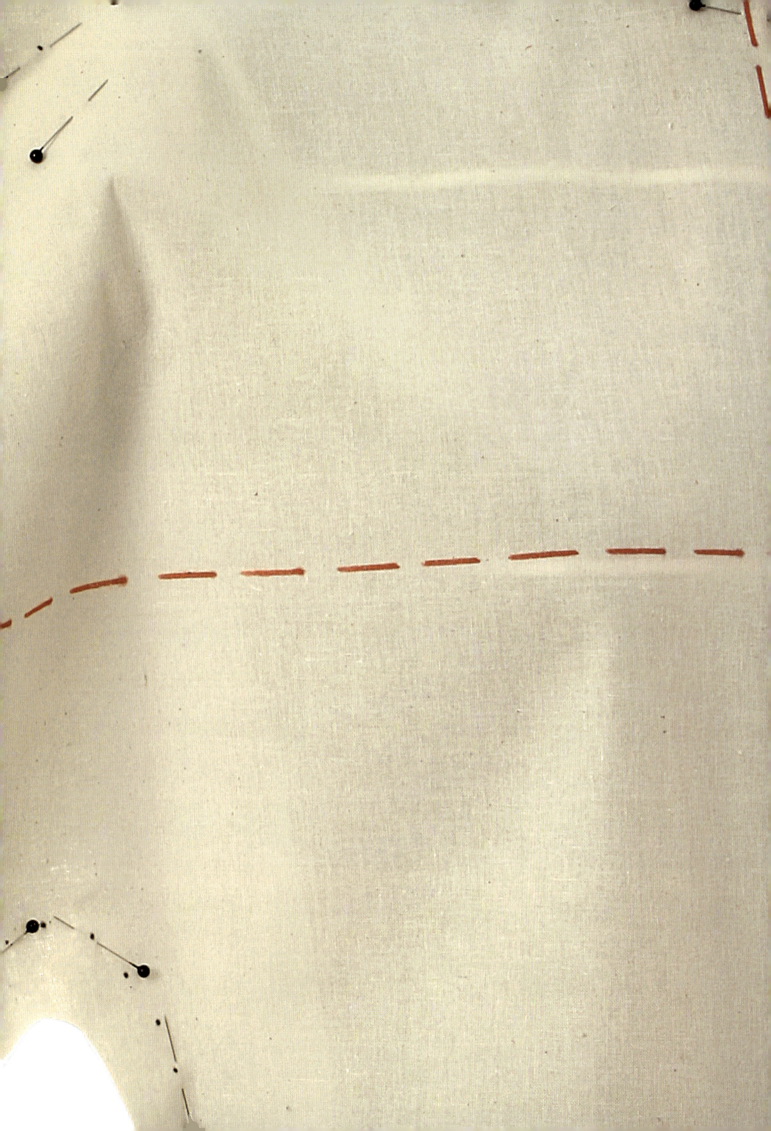

> **0225** > Pin the side seam and the inner arm seam in a nice line towards the wrist. >> Take care that the model is not pulled too tightly across the bust and back. >> Mark the following lines: neck, upper sleeve seam, inner sleeve seam, side seam and sleeve length. >> Remove the whole piece from the stand and true all the lines. >> Cut out the panels with seam allowance.
> **0226** > Pin the panels together flat and check the model on the stand. >> If there is still tension on the inner sleeve seam, then cut into the seam allowance.

Variations:
> Sleeve all-in-one with the bodice
> Cardin sleeve

VARIATIONS

Sleeve all-in-one with the bodice (or drop shoulder style) >

Hang the arm on the stand and use a tape to hang the wrist in the desired position. >> Drape a front and back panel according to your own design. Pin the panels together flat. The shoulder seam is pinned through across the raised arm. >> Pin the panels onto the stand. > **0227 / 0228 / 0229** > Use tape to indicate the shape of the arm hole/sleeve part.

0227 0228 0229

Cardin sleeve > Shoulder padding is used in this sleeve (see p. 37).
>> Attach this first to the stand before draping the panel. >> Drape a front and back panel according to your own design. Clearly mark the arm hole.
>> Prepare a one-piece or two-piece sleeve. >> Hang the arm on the stand.
>> Pin the panels together flat and place this on the stand.

> **0230** > Pin the lower sleeve into the panel, from FSC to BSC. Make nicks in the sleeve at these points. >> Lay the toile smoothly up across the arm hole and affix with pins. >> Pin the shoulder seam and the arm hole.
> **0231** > Pin the round seam onto the head of the sleeve at the end of the shoulder padding. >> Cut away surplus fabric. >> Mark the following lines: shoulder seam, the curve on the head and the arm hole of the sleeve.
>> Remove the sleeve from the stand and true all the lines. > **0232** > Cut out the sleeve with seam allowance.
> **0233** > Pin the sleeve together and check it on the stand.

0230

0231

0233

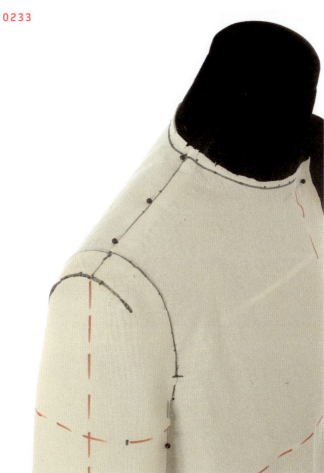

0232

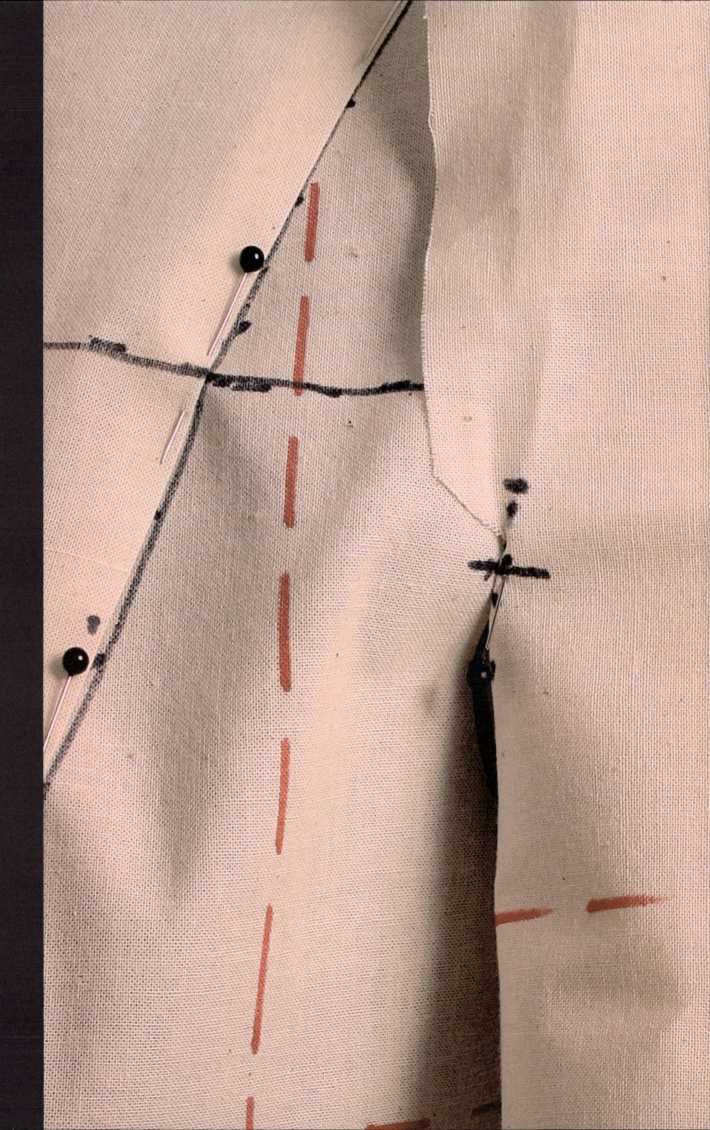

8 COLLARS

BASIC FORMS

Flat collar > This collar runs from CF to CB. >> Drape a front and back panel. Pin the panels together. Place the panels on the stand. >> Deepen the neckline of the panel and clearly indicate the new neckline. CB is deepened to a maximum of half the CF but never more than 0.5 cm. In this example the neck is deepened CF 1 cm, shoulder 1 cm and CB 0.5 cm. **> 0234 >** Prepare the toile as in the example shown.

0234

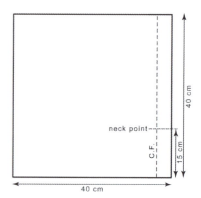

0235

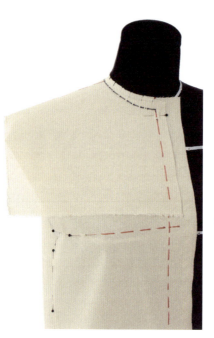

> 0235 > Pin the CF of the collar part to CF on the stand. >> Lay the fabric smoothly across the front panel and the shoulder to CB. >> Cut out the neckline and make nicks in the seam allowance. >> Adhere to the deepened neckline.

0236

0237

> 0236 / 0237 > Use a piece of tape to indicate the shape of the collar. >> This line can be plotted according to your own design. >> Mark the following lines: CF, neckline, CB, shoulder point (control point) and the shape line. >> Remove the collar from the panel and true the lines. >> Cut out the collar with seam allowance and check it on the panel.

Collar stand > This collar runs from CF to CB.
> 0238 > Prepare the toile as in the example shown and cut out the collar with seam allowance. The stand is cut on the straight grain.

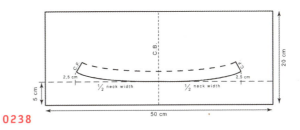

0238

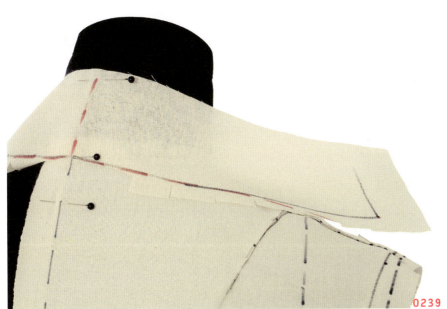

0239
0240

> 0239 / 0240 > Place a front and back panel on the stand. >> Pin the panels together and deepen the neckline, marking this clearly. >> Drape the collar from CB to CF. >> Starting at CB pin the collar onto the neckline with the seam allowance folded inwards.

> 0241 / 0242 > Continue to form the collar in this way through to CF. >> On the shoulder a bit more fabric will have to be folded in to keep the stand of the collar upright. >> Fold the collar inwards at the top and front in order to determine the form. >> Mark the following lines: CF, neckline, shoulder point (control point) and the top of the collar. >> Remove the collar from the panel and true the lines. >> Mirror the other half. >> Cut out the collar with seam allowance and check it on the panel.

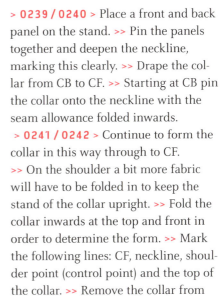

0241   0242

Collar and stand in one piece > Deepen the neckline on the panel and mark it clearly. >> In this example a whole collar is draped. > **0243** > Prepare the toile as in the example shown. The collar is drawn on the bias. >> A collar cut on the bias falls more supply and prevents kinks in the break line.

0243

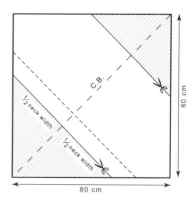

0244

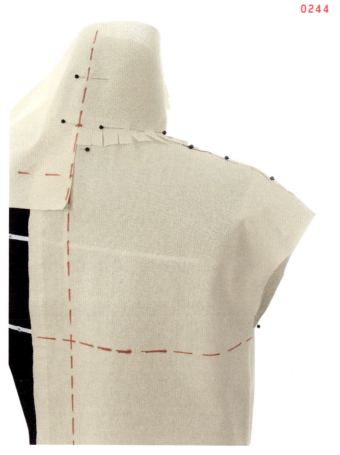

> **0244** > Place a front and back panel on the stand. >> Pin the panels together flat and deepen the neckline, marking this clearly. >> Drape the collar from CB to CF. >> Starting at CB pin the collar onto the neckline with the seam allowance outside. >> Cut in the seam allowance.

> **0245** > Pin the collar through to CF. > **0246** > Fold the collar and determine the form. >> Mark the following lines: CF, neckline, shoulder point (control point) and shape line. >> Remove the collar from the panel and true the lines. >> Mirror the other half and cut out the collar with seam allowance. > **0247** > Check the collar on the panel.

0245

0256   **0247**

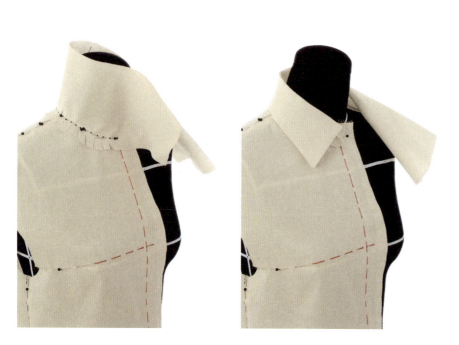

Basic forms:

> Collar and stand in one piece

> Collar with separate stand

Collar with separate stand > The procedure for the stand is the same as for the collar stand. >> An average stand is 2.5 to 3 cm high. >> Place a front and back panel on the stand. >> Pin the panels together flat and deepen the neckline, marking this clearly.

0248

0249   > 0248 > Prepare the toile as in the example >> Mark the stand on the straight grain. **Stand** > 0249 > Starting at CB pin the collar onto the neckline with the seam allowance folded inwards. >> Continue to form the collar in this way through to 1.5 cm past CF (overlap). >> On the shoulder a bit more fabric will have to be folded in to keep the stand of the collar upright. >> Fold the collar inwards at the top and front to determine the form. >> Mark the following lines: CF, overlap, neckline, shoulder point (control point) and the top of the collar. >> Remove the collar from the panel and true the lines. >> Mirror the other half. Cut out the stand with seam allowance. >> Put the stand on the panel. >> Measure the upper ring of the stand from CF to CB.

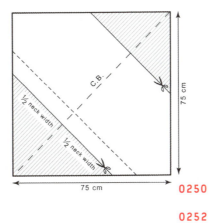

0250

0251

0252

Collar segment > 0250 > Prepare the collar segment according to the example shown - this is cut on the bias in order to achieve a supple fall.

> 0251 > Pin the collar behind the stand at CB and continue its form piece by piece. Make enough nicks here.
> 0252 > Fold the collar down and check the position. >> Determine the form of the collar. >> Take care that the collar falls across the neckline of the stand and that the CB of the collar corresponds to the CB of the panel. >> Mark the following lines: CF, join line and shape line. >> Remove the collar from the stand and true all the lines. >> Mirror the other half and cut out the collar segment with seam allowance. >> Check the collar on the panel.

Notched collar > Overlap, lapel roll line and button > **0253** > Drape half a front panel and half a back panel and pin them together. >> Draw 5-10 cm on CF instead of 4 cm. The extra amount of fabric depends on the size of the overlap and the lapel that is going to be made. >> Pin the panels together flat. >> Deepen the neck at the shoulder and the CB, for example 1 cm on the shoulder and 0.5 cm CB.

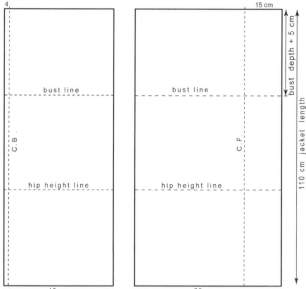

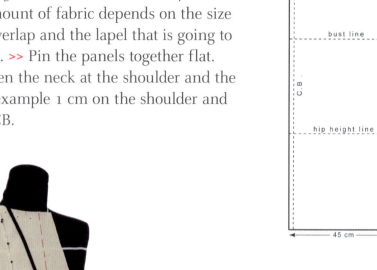

> **0254** > Place the top button on CF at the desired place. >> For a double-breasted overlap this is past the CF line and so more overlap is drawn on CF. >> Cut into the overlap 0.5 cm above the buttonhole and half the button width from the button. >> Fold the overlap in under this point and iron it flat. >> Fold down the lapel and fold in the break line to ± 7 cm under the shoulder seam (shown here by the black tape).

0254

0255

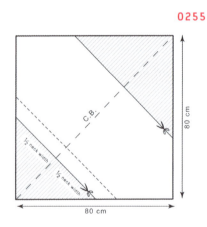

0256

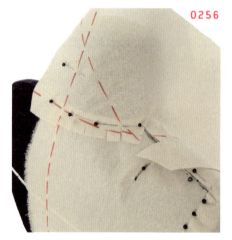

> **0255** > Prepare the collar segment on the bias as shown in the example. >> A collar cut on the bias falls more supply and prevents kinks in the break line. > **0256** > Pin the collar at CB onto the deepened neckline and turn the fabric forwards, making enough nicks so that the collar stands up loosely like a sheath against the neck (not too tight against it).

0257

> **0257** > Continue working in this way as far as ± 2 to 4 cm past the shoulder seam parallel to the break line. >> Indicate this control point (corner point) on the collar and the lapel. >> Now place the collar smoothly onto the lapel part of the front panel and affix with pins.

> Collar and lapel

Basic forms:

> **0258** > Fold collar and lapel together around the break line. The break line runs somewhat diagonally in a straight line from the neck to the top button.

> **0259** > Use tape to determine the shape of the lapel and collar. >> Mark the following lines: join line, shoulder point (control point), collar segment and the shape line of the lapel. >> Remove the collar from the stand and true all the lines.

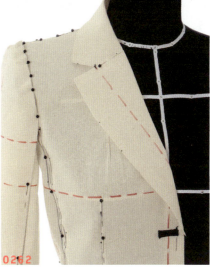

> **0260 / 0261** > Fold back the lapel and adopt the shape line on the inside of the lapel. >> Draw this line through to the corner point and connect it to the shoulder neck point. Draw this corner clearly. >> Cut the corner from the panel with seam allowance. >> Cut out the collar and lapel with seam allowance.

> **0262** > Pin the collar into the panel and check the model on the stand. >> Make sure that the CB of the collar lies at CB of the panel.

Shawl collar > The shawl collar can be draped in two ways.
Example 1 > Set in collar >> For this collar the same procedure is followed as for the notched collar (see p. 110). **>>** The top collar and facing are cut from a single piece of fabric.
Example 2 > Shawl collar all-in-one with bodice > 0263 >
Prepare the toile as in the example shown. **>>** Drape a front and back panel and attach the piece of toile to the top of the front panel. The shoulder dart in the front panel is laid under the collar. **>>** Deepen the neckline on the shoulder and CB.

0263

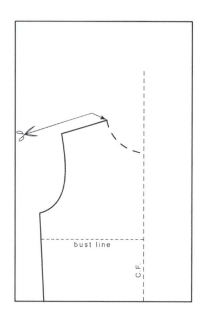

0264

> **0264 >** Pin the front and back panel together flat. **>>** Place the top button at the desired place on CF. **>>** Cut into the overlap 0.5 cm above the buttonhole and half the button width from the button. **>>** Fold the overlap in under the buttonhole and iron it flat.
> **0265 >** Make a nick exactly as far as the deepened neckline.

0265

> **0266 >** Fold down the lapel and iron down the break line to ± 7 cm under the shoulder seam. **>>** Lay the back part of the collar across the shoulder to CB and determine the position of the stand by turning it up or down. **>>** Work from the shoulder to CB.

0266

Basic forms:

> *Shawl Collar*

0267

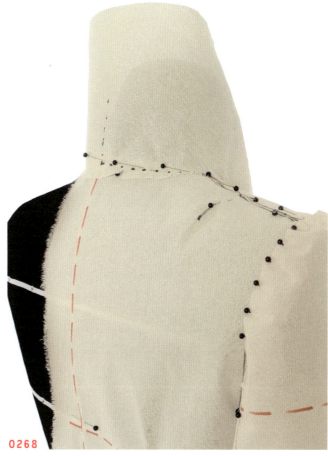

0268

> **0267 / 0268** > Pin the collar in the desired position onto the back neckline, making nicks in the seam allowance so that the collar runs smoothly along the neck like a sheath (not too tight against it).

0269

0270

> **0269 / 0270** > Fold down the shawl collar and use tape to indicate the desired shape. >> Mark the following lines: join line, shape line and CB. >> Remove the whole piece from the stand and true all the lines. >> Cut out the shawl collar with seam allowance and check the model on the stand.

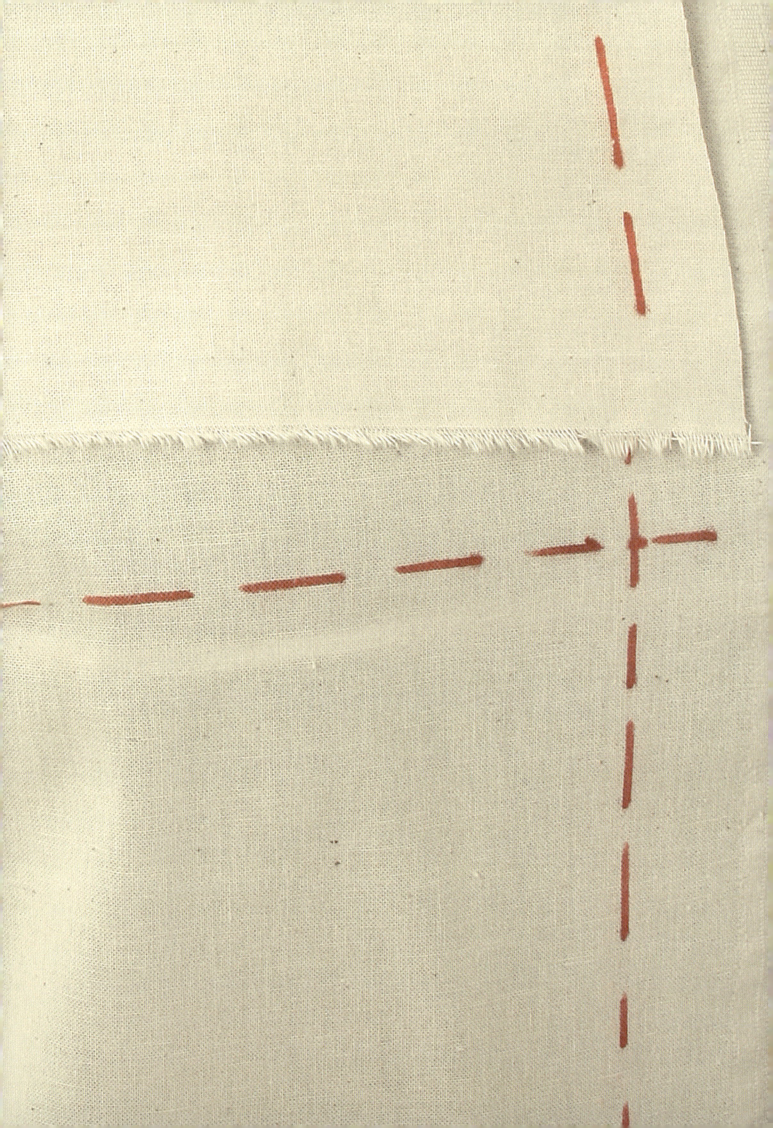

VARIATIONS

Fluted collar > **0271** > Prepare the toile as shown in the example and indicate the CF line.

Variations:
> Fluted collar
> Collar all-in-one with bodice
> Large collar in spacious neckline

0272

0273

0271

> **0272** > Pin the CF of the collar to CF of the panel. >> Turn the collar down so that a flute is created and affix this to the panel. >> Cut out the neckline piece by piece and make nicks in the seam allowance. >> Do not cut too much away at one time. >> Repeat this procedure as far as CB: turn, affix flute, smooth down neckline. >> Determine the form of the collar as you see fit.
> **0273** > Mark the following lines: CF, CB, neckline and the shape of the collar. >> Remove the whole piece from the stand and true all the lines. >> Cut out the collar with seam allowance and check the model on the stand.

Collar all-in-one with bodice > Prepare a front and back panel (see p. 71). > **0274** > Pin the shoulder seams together, running diagonally upwards along the neck. >> Determine the height and form of the collar. >> Mark the following lines: CF, shoulder and shape line of the collar. >> Remove the whole piece from the stand and true all the lines. >> Cut out the panels with seam allowance. >> Pin the panels together flat and check the model on the stand.

0274

Large collar in spacious neckline > First drape a front and back panel and pin the panels together flat. >> Deepen the neckline according to your own design.
Stand > **0275** > Prepare the toile with lengthwise grain as shown in the example.

0275

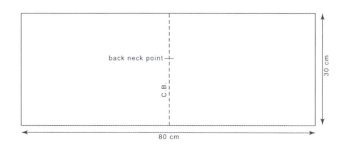

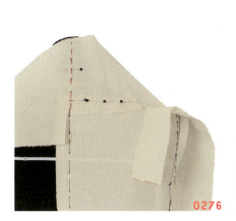

0276 0277 0278

0279

> **0276 / 0277 / 0278** > Pin the CB of the stand onto the deepened neckline with the seam outside. >> Make nicks in the seam allowance and form the stand in the correct position as far as CF. >> Determine the height of the stand. >> Mark the following lines: CF, CB, neckline, shoulder point (control point) and shape line. >> Remove the stand from the panel and true all the lines. Iron adhesive cotton or interfacing behind the stand to give it extra strength. >> Cut out the stand with seam allowance on the join line. > **0279** > Pin the stand onto the neckline.

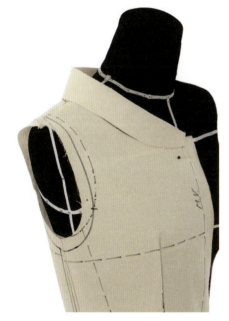

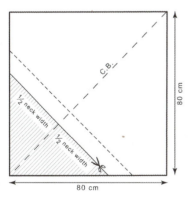

0280

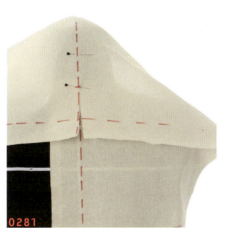

0281

0282

Collar > **0280** > Prepare the toile on the bias as shown above. >> A collar cut on the bias falls more supply and prevents kinks in the break line.

> **0281** > Pin the CB line on the CB of the stand in the same way as the stand. >> Form the collar through to the front by laying the fabric smoothly along the join line of the stand and fastening it with pins. >> Cut away surplus fabric. > **0282** > Fold down the collar and use tape to determine the shape of the outer ring, then fold over or cut away. >> Mark the following lines: CF, CB, join line and the shape line. >> Remove the collar from the stand and true all the lines. >> Cut out the collar with seam allowance. >> Check the collar on the collar stand.

9 COATS AND JACKETS

BASIC FORMS

Fitted coat > **Front panel** > **0283** > Prepare the toile as shown in the example. Height: measure the front length of the coat from the shoulder neck point and add + 5 cm extra. **>>** Indicate the following lines on the toile: **>>** CF + 10-15 cm from the edge of the fabric for the overlap. **>>** Indicate the BW and HH line in the front and back panel. CB lies 4 cm from the edge of the fabric.

0283

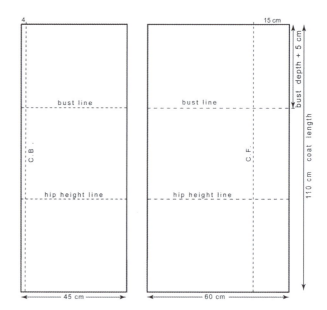

> **0284 / 0285** > Pin the CF, BW and HH line onto the corresponding lines of the stand. **>>** Cut out the neckline and make nicks in the seam allowance. **>>** Fasten the fabric to the shoulder neck point. **>>** Pin the shoulder dart which lies halfway along the shoulder width and runs to ± 2 cm above the bust point. **>>** If the dress stand has shoulder pieces then space will be visible beside the arm hole. Cut away some of the fabric, but not too much. **>>** There is always a small bubble just next to the bust because of the body's curve. **>>** Pin the side seam straight down in front of the tape. **>>** Pin the space at the waist into a dart going down in line with the shoulder dart, starting ± 2 cm under the bust point and approximately in the middle of the front panel, following the contour of the body.

Back panel > **0286** > Pin CB, BW and HH line onto the corresponding lines of the stand. **>>** The back panel is draped in the same way as the front panel. **>>** Make a ± 7 cm shoulder dart half way along the shoulder line, corresponding to the shoulder dart in the front panel. **>>** Pin the waist dart in line with the shoulder dart so that it runs approximately in the middle of the back panel, following the contour of the body. **>>** Pin the shoulder and side seams together.

0287

0288

0289

0290

0291

> **0287** > Mark the following lines: CF, CB, neckline, waistline, darts, shoulder seam, side seam and arm hole.
>> Remove the whole piece from the stand and true all the lines. >> If necessary mark extra width on the side seam and the arm hole (see p. 41)
> **0288** > Indicate the FSC and BSC on the panel. The FSC lies 9.5 cm from the side seam and the BSC 7.5 cm from the side seam. >> Cut out the panels with seam allowance. >> Pin the panels together flat and check the model on the stand. >> If there is still tension on a seam or dart then cut into the seam allowance.

Sleeve > 0289 / 0290 / 0291 > Drape a sleeve according to your own design. >> This example shows a two-piece sleeve (see p. 96)

Collar > A collar of your own design can be draped on a coat. This example shows a notched collar (see p. 110)

Details > Place any details on the model. Decide on the length of the coat.

Waisted coat > 0292 > This model consists of four panels on a half model. The panels are waisted and are wider at the hem. **>>** Prepare the toile as shown in the example. **>>** Indicate the following lines on the toile: **>>** CF + 10-15 cm from the edge of the fabric for the overlap. **>>** Indicate the BW and HH line. CB lies 4 cm from the edge of the fabric. **>>** Draw a vertical grain line in the middle of panels 2 and 3.

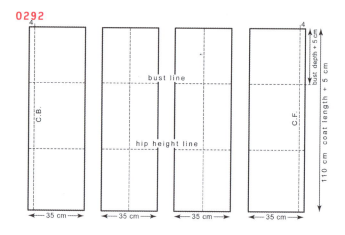

0292

0293

0294

0295

> 0293 > In this example shoulder padding is pinned onto the stand. **>>** Apply tapes to the front and back of the stand to show where the shape lines (seams) come.

Front panels > Panel 1 > 0294 > Pin the CF, BW and HH line onto the corresponding lines of the stand. **>>** Cut out the neckline, make nicks in the seam allowance and fasten the shoulder to the halfway point.

Panel 2 > 0295 > Pin the second panel onto the stand, the BW and HH lines on the corresponding lines of the stand. Make sure the vertical grain line remains straight. **>>** Fasten the shoulder and cut away excess toile next to the arm hole. **>>** Pin the seam together. This seam runs in a flowing line from the shoulder across the bust point to the waist and with more width to the hem. Pin the same amount of hem space in both panels.

Back panels > 0296 / 0297 > Panel 4 > Begin CB. This panel is draped in the same way as panel 1. **Panel 3 >** Pin the third panel onto the stand. This is draped in the same way as panel 2. Connect the shoulder seam to the seam on the front panel. >> Pin the seam together. This seam runs in a flowing line from the shoulder to the waist and down with more width to the hem. Pin the same amount of hem space in both panels. >> Pin the shoulder seam to-

gether. >> Pin the side seam of the front and back panels together. The seam runs down to the hem with extra with. >> Mark the following lines: CF, CB, neckline, waistline, component seams, shoulder seam, side seam and arm hole. >> Remove the whole piece from the stand and true all the lines. >> If necessary mark extra width on the side seam and the arm hole (see p. 41). >> Indicate the front sleeve cross mark (FSC) and back sleeve cross mark (BSC) in the arm hole on the panel. The FSC lies 9.5 cm from the side seam and the BSC 7.5 cm from the side seam. >> Cut out the panels with seam allowance. >> Pin the panels together flat and check the model on the stand. >> If there is still tension on a seam then cut into the seam allowance. >> Decide on the length of the coat.

0296

0297

0298

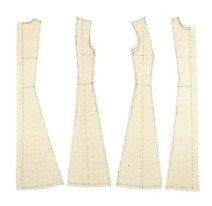

0299

0300

0301

> 0299 / 0300 / 0301 > Collar > Deepen the neckline. >> Drape a collar according to your own design. This example shows a collar and stand in one piece (see p. 108). **Sleeve >** Drape a sleeve according to your own design. >> This example shows a two-piece sleeve (see p. 96). **Details >** Place any details on the model, such as a pocket flap.

Flared coat > 0302 > Prepare the toile as shown in the example. Indicate the following lines on the toile: **>>** CF + 4 cm from the edge of the fabric for the overlap. **>>** Indicate the BW and HH line in the front and back panel. CB lies 4 cm from the edge of the fabric.

0302

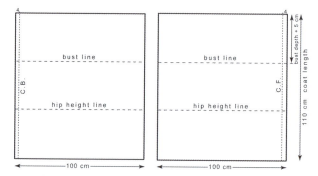

0303

Front panel > 0303> Place shoulder padding on the stand if needed (see p. 37). **>>** Pin the CF, BW and HH line onto the corresponding lines of the stand. **>>** Cut out the neckline and make nicks in the seam allowance. **>>** Pin the shoulder neck point. **>>** Place the first flare starting at the bust. Let the toile drop a little on the shoulder and fasten the flare. **>>** Pin the beginning of the shoulder. **>>** Lay a second flare next to the bust and let the toile drop a little on the shoulder before fastening the flare. **>>** Pin the rest of the shoulder. **>>** You can turn a flare at various places in the front panel.

0304

Back panel > 0304> Pin the CB, BW and HH line onto the corresponding lines of the stand. **>>** It is possible to turn the CB line of the toile past the CB of the stand so as to create more fluting in the back panel. **>>** Cut out the neckline and make nicks in the seam allowance. **>>** Turn a flare in the panel from the shoulder neck point and fasten it. **>>** Pin the first part of the shoulder **>>** Turn the next flare in the back panel and fasten it. You can turn several or larger flares in the back panel. Take care that the amount of space in the back panel is no less than in the front panel. **>>** Fasten the rest of the shoulder. **>>** Pin together the side seam of the front and back panel. Make sure that the side seam runs down in a straight line. **>>** Mark the following lines: CF, CB, neckline, shoulder seam, hipline, side seam and arm hole.

>> Remove the whole piece from the stand and true all the lines.

>> Determine the width of the overlap.

>> If necessary mark extra width on the side seam and the arm hole (see p. 41). **>>** Indicate the FSC and BSC in the arm hole on the panel. The FSC lies 9.5 cm from the side seam and the BSC 7.5 cm from the side seam. **>>** Cut out the panels with seam allowance. **>>** Pin the panels together flat and check the model on the stand.

0305

0306

> 0305 / 0306 > Collar > Deepen the neckline. **>>** Drape a collar according to your own design. This example shows a collar and stand in one piece (see p. 108). **Sleeve >** Drape a sleeve according to your own design. **>>** This example shows a Cardin sleeve (see p. 103). **Details >** Place any details on the model and decide on the length.

Blazer with side panel > 0307 > Prepare the toile as shown in the example. **>>** Indicate the following lines on the toile: **>>** CF + 15-20 cm from the edge of the fabric for the overlap and shawl collar. **>>** Indicate the BW and HH line in the front and back panel. CB lies 4 cm from the edge of the fabric.

0307

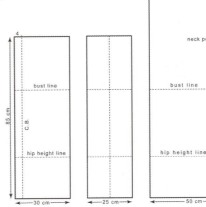

0308

0309

Front panel > 0308 / 0309 > Pin the CF, BW and HH line onto the corresponding lines of the stand. **>>** Do not cut out the neckline yet. **>>** First fasten the shoulder neck point with pins. **>>** Then pin the shoulder dart which lies closer to the neck and CF so that the dart ends up lying under the shawl collar. **>>** Cut away surplus fabric on the shoulder and next to the arm hole. **>>** Fasten the panel next to the bust at BW and HH. **>>** Pin the waist dart.

Back panel > 0310 > Pin the CB, BW and HH line onto the corresponding lines of the stand. **>>** Cut out the neckline and make nicks in the seam allowance. **>>** Pin the shoulder dart midway on the shoulder. **>>** If there is to be a seam at CB in the final model then the CB line can be laid a little across CB of the stand at waist height. **>>** Pin the waist dart in line with the shoulder dart.

0310

0311

0312

0313

Side panel > 0311 / 0312 / 0313 > Pin the grain line straight on the stand. **>>** Pin the seams on the front and back together where you wish.

0314

> **0314 / 0315 / 0316** > Mark the following lines: CF, CB, back neckline, shoulder seam, side seams, darts, arm hole and the shape on the front and the bottom. >> Remove the whole piece from the stand and true all the lines.

0315

>> If necessary mark extra width on the two side seams and the arm hole (see p. 41). >> Cut out the panels with seam allowance. Leave the extra fabric for the shawl collar on the front panel. >> Indicate the FSC and BSC in the

0316

arm hole on the panel. The FSC lies 9.5 cm from the side seam and the BSC 7.5 cm from the side seam.
>> Pin the panels together flat and check the model on the stand.

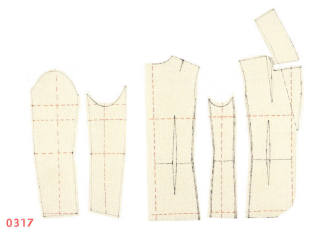

0317

Collar > **0317 / 0318** > Drape a collar according to your own design. This example shows a shawl collar (see p. 112).
Sleeve > Drape a sleeve according to your own design. This example shows a two-piece sleeve (see p. 96)

0318

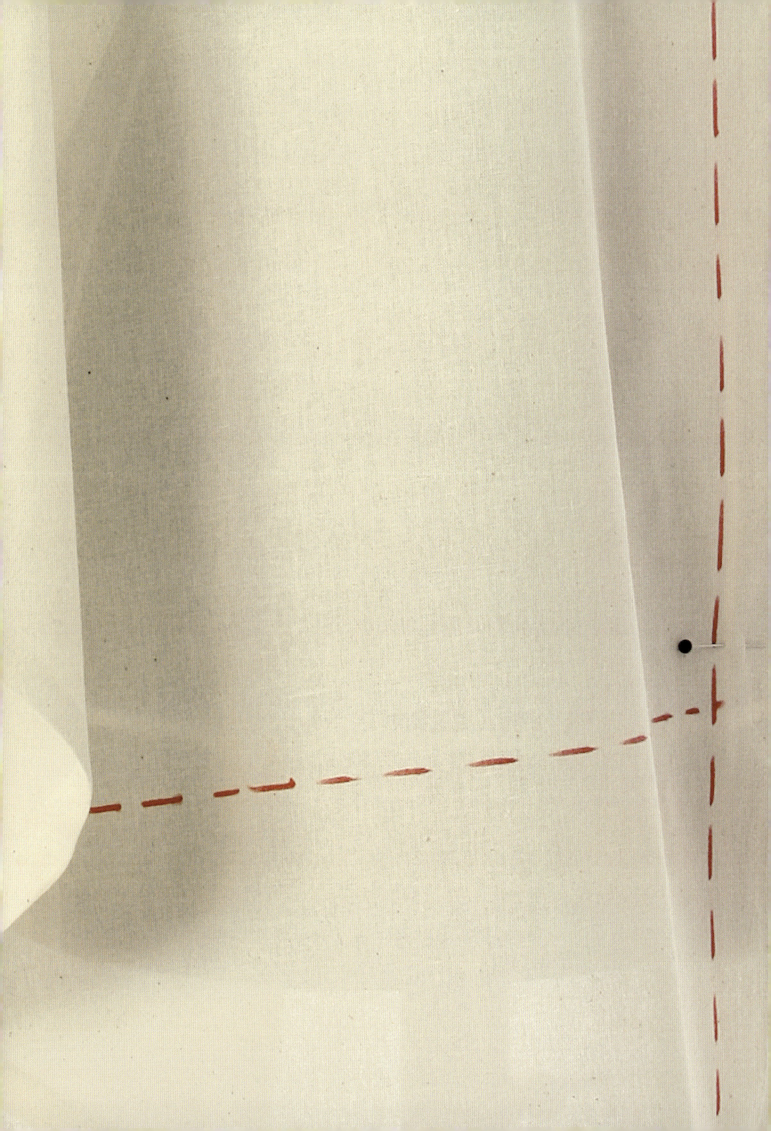

VARIATIONS

Cape > Hang the arm of the stand in the desired position. The more the arm is raised the more space is created in the cape.

> 0319 > Prepare the toile as shown in the example. Height: measure the front length from the shoulder neck point and add 5 cm extra. **>>** Width is measured from the overlap as far as the wrist **>>** Indicate the following lines on the toile: **>>** CF + 4 cm from the edge of the fabric. **>>** Indicate the BW and HH line in the front and back panel. CB lies 4 cm from the edge of the fabric.

0319

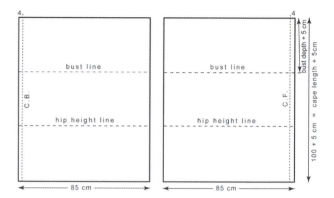

Front panel > 0320 > Pin the CF, BW and HH line onto the corresponding lines of the stand. **>>** Cut out the neckline and make nicks in the seam allowance. **>>** Fasten the shoulder neck point. **>>** For extra flaring turn the fabric down a little at the shoulder and fasten it. **>>** Affix the toile to the upper arm seam and cut away surplus fabric.
Back panel > Pin the CB, BW and HH line onto the corresponding lines of the stand. **>>** Cut out the neckline and make nicks in the seam allowance.
>> Fasten the shoulder neck point.
>> Pin the beginning of the shoulder and turn a flare in the back panel and then fasten it. Fasten the rest of the shoulder and the upper arm seam.
>> Pin front and back panels together on the upper arm seam. **>>** Cut away excess toile.

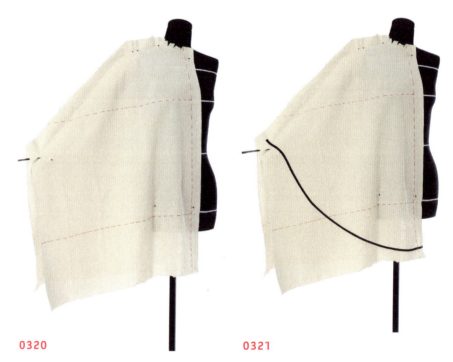

0320

0321

> 0321 > Use black tape on the front and back panel to indicate the shape of the hem. There are many possible variations. **>>** Mark the following lines: CF, CB, neckline, shoulder seam/upper arm seam as far as the wrist and the shape line of the hem. **>>** Remove the whole piece from the stand and true all the lines. **>>** Cut out the panels with seam allowance. **>>** Pin the panels together flat and check the model on the stand.

Collar > 0322 / 0323 / 0324 > Deepen the neckline. **>>** Drape a collar according to your own design. This example shows a high collar from CF to CB (see p. 107).

0322

0323   0324

Trench coat > Prepare the toile according to work drawing. **0283 >>** Take extra fabric width for a pleat CB (in this example about 10 cm).

0325

Front panel > 0325 > Pin the CF and BW lines onto the corresponding lines of the stand. **>>** Cut out the neckline and make nicks in the seam allowance. **>>** Pin the fabric smoothly across the shoulder. **>>** Pin the side seam in front of the tape to make extra space in the front panel. **>>** Cut away part of the arm hole.

0326

Back panel > 0326 > In this model a pleat 5 cm deep is laid next to CB. **>>** Prepare the toile, iron the pleat in it before pinning the toile to the stand. **>>** Pin the CB and BW lines onto the corresponding lines of the stand. **>>** Cut out the neckline and make nicks in the seam allowance. **>>** Pin the fabric smoothly across the shoulder. **>>** Pin the side seam in front of the tape to make extra space in the back panel. **>>** Cut away part of the arm hole.

0327

> **0327 >** Pin the shoulder seam and the side seam together.
> **0328 >** Use tape to indicate the raglan shape and the arm hole. The arm hole needs to be deepened.

0328

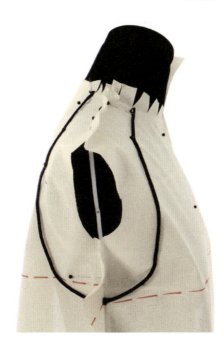

0329

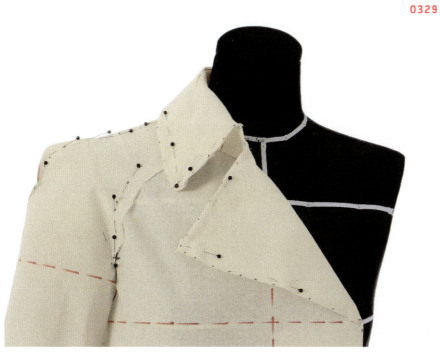

Sleeve and collar > 0329 > For raglan sleeve see p. 98. **>>** Here the one-piece sleeve is used. **>>** In the final model the shoulder seam can be extended across the upper arm and incorporated as an upper arm seam. **>>** A collar with stand has been draped on this model (see p. 109). **>>** Deepen the neckline before draping the collar. **>>** Indicate the desired form of the collar and lapel.

> **0330** > A yoke piece is draped over the front panel and fastened at the raglan shape, neck and arm hole. **>>** Take a piece of toile and indicate the straight grain lengthwise and crosswise. **>>** Pin the piece onto the front panel.

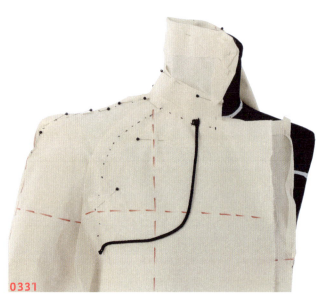

0331

0332

> **0331** > Mark the raglan shape and the neckline and cut them out with seam allowance. **>>** Use tape to indicate the shape of the yoke piece.

> **0332** > A yoke piece a bit wider than the coat is also draped over the back panel. **>>** Prepare a toile with a CB. **>>** This yoke piece is also fastened at the neckline, raglan shape and side seam. **>>** Mark the neckline, raglan shape and side seam and cut them out with seam allowance. **>>** Remove the whole piece from the stand and true all the lines. **>>** Pin the panels together flat and check the model on the stand.

0333   0334

> **0333 / 0334 >** Lastly, place the details on the model, such as a pocket, epaulet and band around the sleeve.

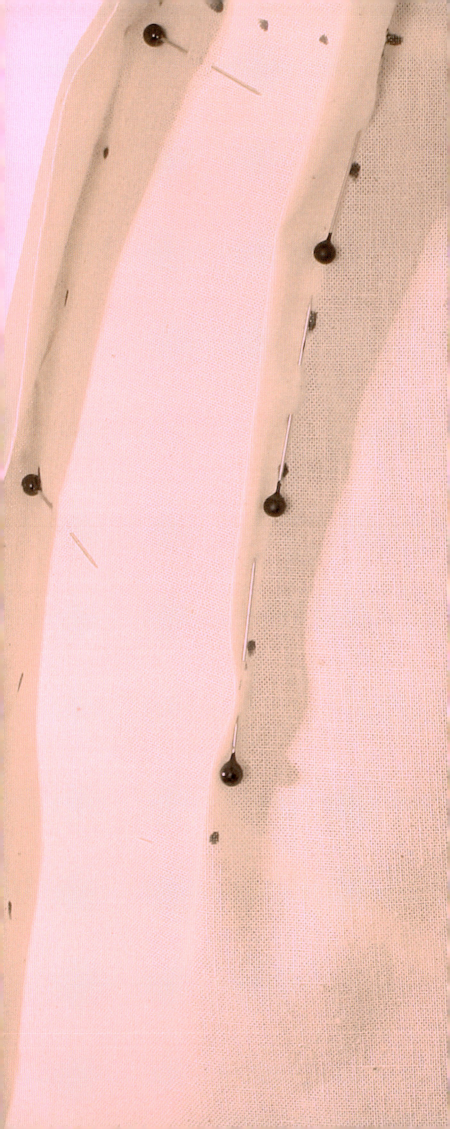

BASIC FORMS

Straight trousers > 0335 > Begin by applying the tapes to the stand (see p. 36). **>>** Prepare the toile as shown in the example. Trouser length + waist seam and hem. Place a vertical grain line in the middle of the panel and indicate the crutch depth line (CD).

0335

crutch depth line

grain line back panel

crutch depth line

grain line front panel

+ 5 cm

crutch depth

125 cm   trouser length

55 cm

55 cm

0336

0337

0338

0339

Front leg > 0336 > Pin the grain line to the balance line on the front of the leg. **>>** Make sure the CD line corresponds with the CD line on the stand. **>>** Fold the bottom inwards and pin the toile to the foot. **>>** Pin CF onto the stand. **> 0337 >** Pin the outside leg seam from the HH line straight down as far as the ankle. Space is created near the ankle because of the form of the leg. **>>** Sweep away as much fabric as possible over the outer leg seam from the CD line to the waist.

> 0338 / 0339 > The space remaining in the waist is pinned together into a dart, as with the straight skirt. **>>** Cut in ± 2 cm above the CD line to CF.

0340

0341

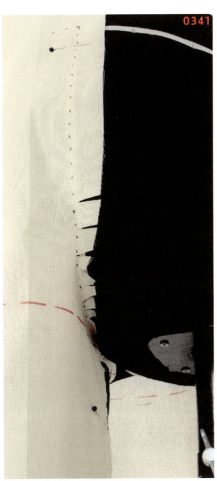

> **0340/0341 >** Fasten CF as far as the HH line. **>>** Cut away surplus fabric at CF. **>>** Cut in the crutch seam and shape this around the leg to the inner leg seam. Make sufficient nicks as far as the crutch seam. **>>** Pin the inside seam down in a straight line. Here too space is created at the ankle because of the form of the leg.

Back leg > 0342 > Pin the grain line to the balance line at the back of the leg. **>>** Make sure that the CD line corresponds with the CD line on the stand. Fold the bottom inwards. **>>** Pin CB onto the CB of the stand. **> 0343 >** Smooth the toile over the CB line. Fasten CB from waist to HH line. **>>** Pin the outside leg seam from waist to CD line, sweeping away as much fabric as possible over the outer leg seam to the waist. **>>** The space remaining in the waist is pinned together into a dart, as with the straight skirt. **>>** Pin the side seam down in a straight line. Space is created at the ankle. **>>** Cut away surplus fabric at CB. **>>** Cut in ± 2 cm above the CD line to CB.

0342

0343

0344

0345

0347

0346

> **0344 / 0345** > Cut in the crutch seam and shape this around the leg to the inner leg seam. Make sufficient nicks as far as the crutch seam.

>> Pin the inside seam down in a straight line. Space is created at the ankle. >> Mark the following lines: CF, CB, darts, waistline, inner leg seam, outer leg seam, knee height line and hem. >> Remove the whole piece from the stand and true all the lines. >> Cut out the panels with seam allowance.

> **0346 / 0347** > Pin the panels together flat and check the model on the stand.

Trousers with fitted leg > **0348** > For trousers with fitted leg a straight pair of trousers is first draped. >> Pin off an equal amount on both sides at the side seam and the inner leg seam. The grain line should continue to run through the middle.

0348

VARIATIONS

Pleated trousers without side seam and with raised waist

> This pair of trousers can have one or more pleats. >> In this example two pleats are made on the front.

> **0349** > Prepare the toile as shown in the example. Place the grain line in the centre of the toile. >> Before you begin iron the pleats and pleat depth in the fabric.

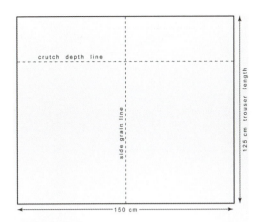

0349

0350   0351

0352   0353

Front panel > 0350 > Pin the grain line in a straight line onto the stand. >> Pin the CD line onto the CD line of the stand. > **0351 >** Pin CF from waistline as far as the HH line. >> Cut away surplus fabric at CF. >> Cut in ± 2 cm above the CD line to CF.
>> Cut in the crutch seam and shape this around the leg to the inner leg seam. Make sufficient nicks. >> Pin the inside seam down in a straight line.

Back panel > 0352 > Smooth the toile over the CB line. Fasten CB from waist to HH line. >> Cut away surplus fabric at CB. >> Cut in ± 2 cm above the CD line to CB. >> Cut in the crutch seam and shape this around the leg to the inner leg seam. Make sufficient nicks. >> Pin the inside seam down in a straight line.

> **0353 >** Pin a dart at the side seam to remove surplus fabric. >> Fold in the pleats, following the contour of the body straight upwards. >> Pin a dart in the back panel.

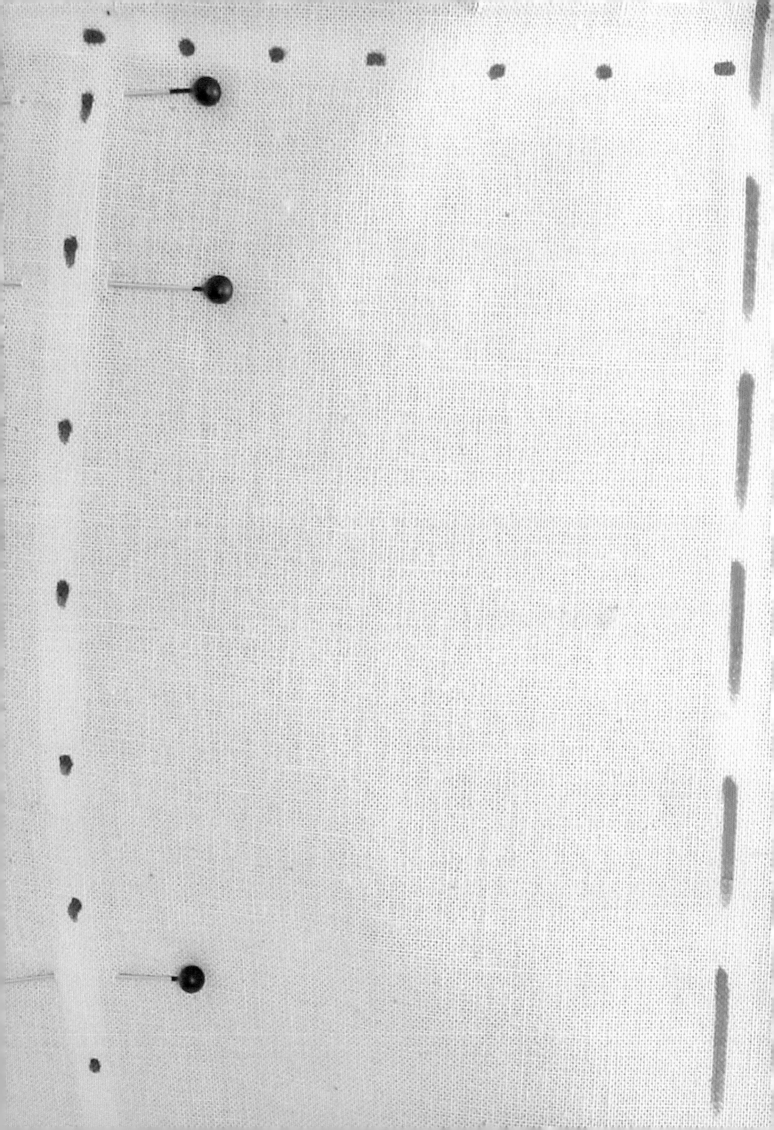

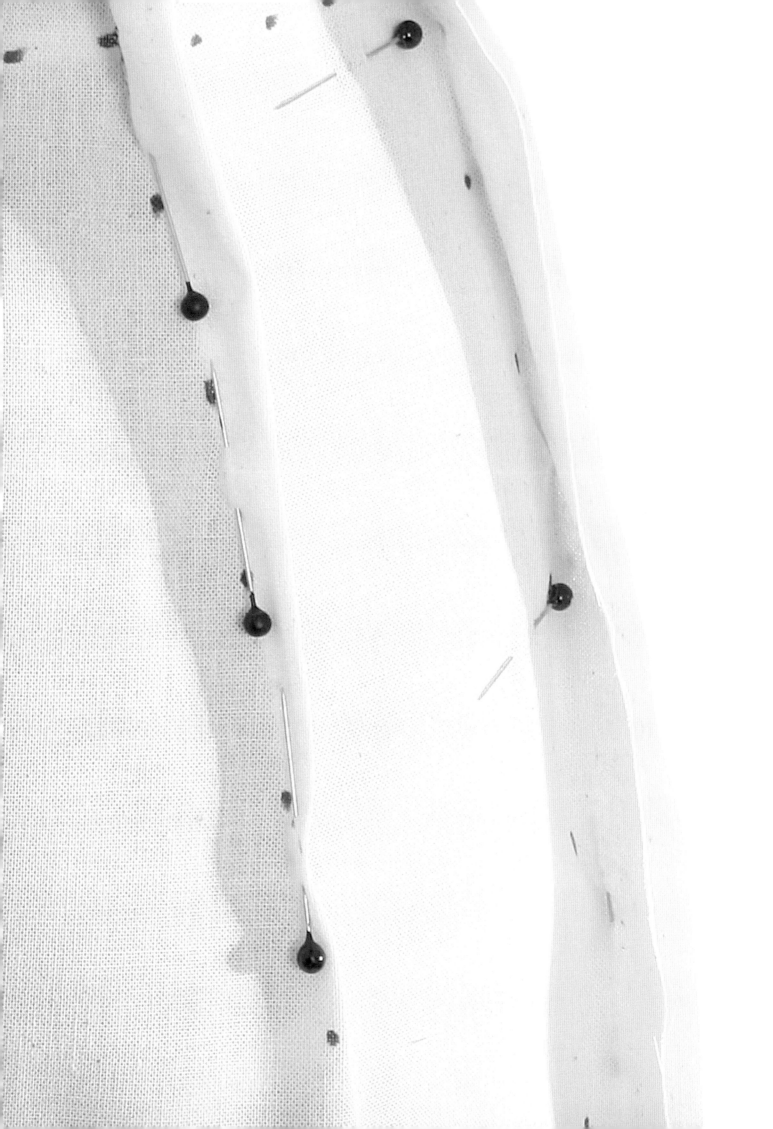

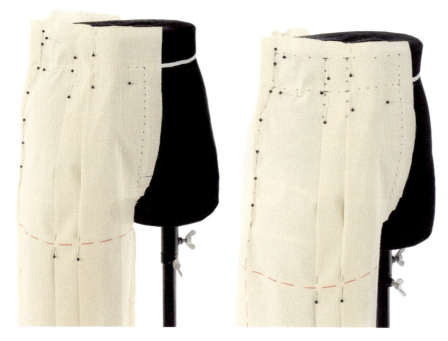

> **0354 / 0355** > Mark the following lines: CF, CB, pleats, darts, waistline, raised waistline, inner leg seam, side seam, knee height line and hem. **>>** Remove the whole piece from the stand and true all the lines. **>>** Cut out the panels with seam allowance. > **0356 / 0357** > Pin the trousers together flat and check the model on the stand.

0356

0357

Hip-huggers > 0358 > For these hip-huggers a pair of trousers is draped as far as the waist.
>> Use black tape to show the shape of the lowered waist and mark this line.

Jodhpurs > 0359 / 0360 / 0361 / 0362 > First place the figure lines on the stand.

0358

0359

0360

0361

0362

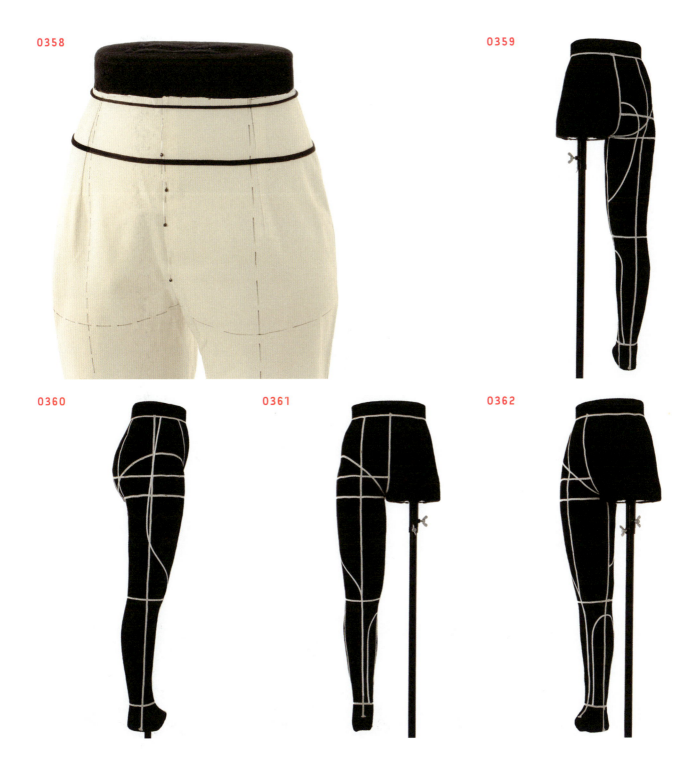

> 0363 > Prepare the five separate panels with straight grain and place a horizontal and vertical grain line on each panel. **>>** Begin with the first small panel for the inside leg. Pin the panel with straight grain onto the stand.
>> Mark the figure line on the panel and cut out the toile with seam allowance.

> 0364 > Pin the second panel with straight grain onto the stand. **>>** Cut out the crutch seam and make nicks in the seam allowance. **>>** Mark the figure line on the panel and cut out the toile with seam allowance.

> 0365 > Pin the third panel with straight grain onto front leg and pin it along the shape line indicated on the first panel. **>>** Mark the figure line on the panel and cut out the toile with seam allowance.

> 0366 > Pin the fourth panel with straight grain onto front leg. **>>** Pin the CD line to the CD line of the stand.
>> Fasten CF from waist as far as the HH line. **>>** Smooth down the space from the CD line and CF to the waist/side seam. **>>** The space remaining in the waist is pinned together into a dart. Cut in ± 2 cm above the CD line to CF.
>> Cut away surplus fabric at CF.
>> Cut in the crutch seam and shape this around the leg to the inner leg seam. Make sufficient nicks. **>>** Pin panel 4 to panel 1, and panel 2 to panel 3 with a bit of space on the front leg.
>> Mark the figure line on the panel and cut out the panel with seam allowance. **>>** Retain enough fabric so you can make the shape of the bulge in the side seam.

0363

0364

0365

0366

> **0367** > Prepare the toile for the fifth panel. The length of the panel is length of trousers + waist seam and hem.
>> Place a vertical grain line in the middle of the panel and mark the CD line. >> Pin the grain line in a straight line onto the stand. >> Smooth the toile over the CB line. Pin CB from waist to HH line. >> The space remaining in the waist is pinned together into a dart.
>> Cut away surplus fabric at CB.
>> Cut in the crutch seam and shape this around the leg to the inner leg seam. Make sufficient nicks.
> **0368** > Pin panel 5 to panels 1, 2, 3 (calf side seam). Pin the side seam to the waist, following the form. >> Mark the following lines: CF, CB, crutch seam, dart, waistline, inner leg seam, outer leg seam, all the panels and the hem. > **0369** > Remove the whole thing from the stand and true all the lines. >> Cut out the panels with seam allowance.
> **0370 / 0371** > Pin the trousers together flat and check the model on the stand.

0367

0368

0369

0370

0371

11 DRAPINGS

Introduction to
draped styles:

INTRODUCTION TO DRAPED STYLES

Draping means arranging the fabric in folds or flares or in order to acquire more space at a particular point, for the purposes of the construction or the design of a garment. >> We can distinguish various sorts of drapings or pleats.

Fixed pleats Fixed pleats have a sharp fold and are pressed in.
Ruffles Ruffles are created by arbitrarily gathering space together.
Draped styles With draped styles the fabric is laid in a particular direction. >> It is best to use a supple toile so that the draping falls well. >> Use the fabric on the bias to promote a supple fall, thus emphasising the forms of the body. >> Draping is often labour-intensive and requires a feeling for form and material.
Waterfall A waterfall is a section of fabric that falls loosely in a particular form and can be cut to the required figure. >> For a stiffer look, a more robust toile can be used. If you want the garment to fall supply then use fabric cut on the bias. >> If a pleat does not fall the way you want it to, remove the

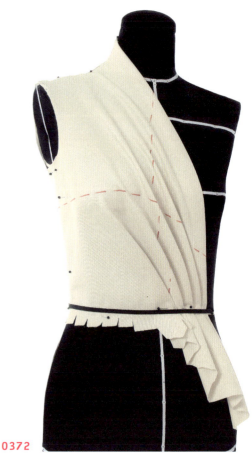

0372

whole piece from the stand and start again. It is recommended to iron the toile again. >> Never force the toile in a particular direction, but let the folds in the fabric fall naturally.
> 0372 > When you have made pleats in a particular place, pin them in, place a tape across the pleats and cut out the panel with seam. >> Always mark the pleats on top and bottom layer, so you can put them back where they are supposed to be. >> In this chapter the draped styles are draped on the stand. The other remaining front and back panels can be interpreted according to your own design.

BODICES

Bodice with waterfall drapery > 0373 > Prepare the toile as shown in the example. >> Mark the following lines on the toile: CF and BW.

0373

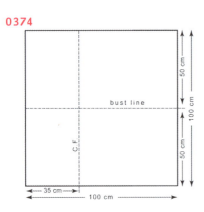

0374

Front panel > 0374 > In this example a bit more fabric is used to start with. >> Pin CF and BW line onto the corresponding lines of the stand. >> Pin the shoulder seam and cut it out with seam allowance as far as the shoulder neck point. >> The space of the shoulder dart is transferred to the waist and pinned together.

> Bodice with
diagonal drapery

Bodices:
> Bodice with
waterfall drapery

Introduction to
draped styles:

11 DRAPINGS
150 - 151

> 0375 / 0376 / 0377 > Turn the fabric forwards and cut the flares into the desired form. **>>** Drape a back panel with a shoulder and waist dart. **>>** Mark the following lines: CB, neckline, waistline, darts, shoulder seam, side seam, arm hole and flares. **>>** Remove the whole piece from the stand and true all the lines. **>>** Mark extra width as desired on the side seam and arm hole. **>>** Cut out the panels with seam allowance. **>>** Pin the panels together flat and check the model on the stand.

0375 **0376** **0377**

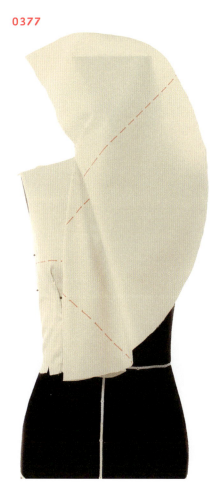

Bodice with diagonal drapery **> 0378 >** Prepare the toile as shown in the example. **>>** Mark the following lines on the toile: CF and BW. **Front panel > 0379 >** Pin CF and BW onto the corresponding lines of the stand. The panel should be pinned higher on the stand because of the upright collar.

0379

0378

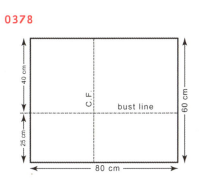

> **0380** > Pin the shoulder line and the curve towards the neck. >> Pin the side seam. >> Divide the space created at the waist into pleats towards CF. >> Stretch the pleats a little for a sharper effect.

> **0381** > Divide the space to the right of CF also into pleats and fold the diagonal line inwards. >> Place a tape in the waist. >> Mark the following lines: CB, waistline, pleats, darts, shoulder seam, side seam and the curve to the neck, side seam, arm hole and the diagonal neckline. >> Remove the whole piece from the stand and true all the lines. >> Mark extra width as desired on the side seam and arm hole. >> Cut out the panels with seam allowance.

>> Pin the panels together flat and check the model on the stand.

Back panel with drapery > Symmetrical draping styles are completely draped so the effect of the folds can be properly seen. **Back panel with drapery > 0382 >** Prepare the toile as shown in the example. >> Mark the following lines on the toile: CB and waistline. >> Leave the point under the waistline on the fabric. **> 0383 >** Fold the toile double at CB and pin off a point at the waistline. The pinned-off line is now the new CB.
>> Cut into the toile at the bottom at CB as far as the waistline.
>> Pin the new CB to the stand from waist to neck.

0382

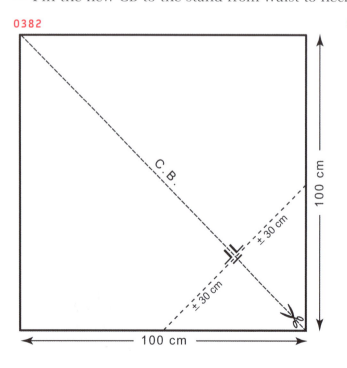

0383

> 0384 / 0385 > Pin the panel smoothly toward the side seam and the shoulder. You will notice that the prepared waistline runs upwards. Cut off surplus fabric under the waistline and make nicks in the seam allowance so the panel can be laid smoothly.

>> Partially pin the shoulder and cut out the arm hole. >> Drape a front panel. This will need a high neckline to prevent the drapes on the back panel from sinking. >> Pin the side seam.

> 0386 > Remove the pins from CB and form the drapes. >> Fold surplus fabric inwards and shape the pleats on the shoulder. >> Mark the following lines: waistline, pleats, shoulder seam, side seam and arm hole. >> Remove the whole piece from the stand and true all the lines. >> Cut out the panels with seam allowance. >> Pin the panels together flat and check the model on the stand.

0384

0385

0386

Corset with drapery **> 0387 >** First make a corset bodice (see pp. 68–70) for attaching the drapery.

> 0388 / 0389 > This drapery is draped onto the bodice with a stretch fabric. The fabric should have a horizontal grain since the stretching of the tricot takes on the shape of the body.

>> Pin the pleats from top to bottom where you want them to be. >> In the finished model the pleats will be fixed to the bodice at the places occupied by the pins.

0389

0387

0388

> 0390 / 0391 > This drapery uses a woven fabric. The fabric is draped on the bias so the pleats can be laid in nicely. **>>** Start at the top and first insert the pleats on the right. Determine the place and amount of pleats as you see fit. **>>** Cut off excess fabric. **>>** Drape the other side. **>>** In the finished model the pleats will be fixed to the bodice at the places occupied by the pins.

0390

0391

SKIRTS

Skirt with asymmetrical draped flounce **> 0392 >** Take an ample amount of fabric for this model. **>>** Prepare the toile as in the example. **> 0393 >** Pin the CF line to the CF of the stand.

0392

0393

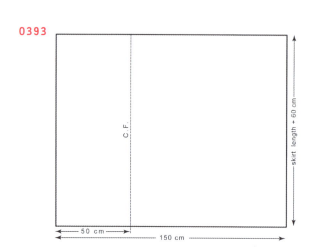

C. F.

skirt length + 60 cm

50 cm

150 cm

> **0394 / 0395>** Place a pin at waist height CF. **>>** Take up an amount of space on the side and attach it to the waistline. Repeat this a few times. The CF turns away at the bottom. **>>** Cut off surplus fabric above the waistline as far as the last pleat.

> **0396 >** Cut the flounce into the desired shape. **>>** Place black tape in the waist to determine the waistline. **>>** Drape a whole back panel from side seam, past the other side seam to half-way along CF (bottom layer). **>>** Decide on the length of the skirt. **>>** Mark the following lines: waistline, pleats, side seam, darts and the shape of the flounce. **>>** Remove the whole piece from the stand and true all the lines.

> **0397 >** Cut out the panels with seam allowance. Take care when cutting the pleats that they are first pinned closed and then cut out with seam. If this is not done carefully the pleats will not hang well. **>>** Pin the panels together flat and check the model on the stand.

0394

0395

0397

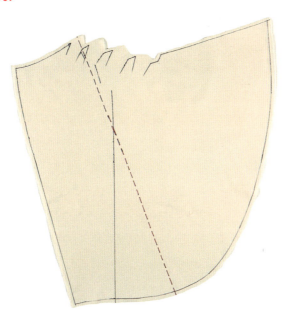

0396

Skirt with crossed drapery > A whole front panel is draped so the effect of the drapery is easy to judge. **> 0398 >** Prepare the toile as shown in the example.

0398

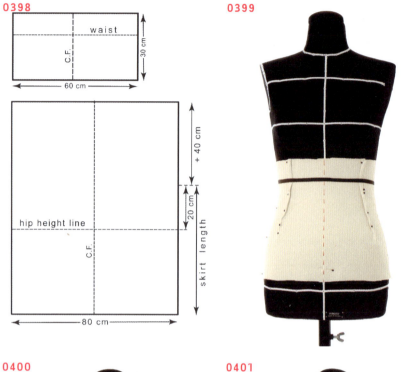

0399

Hip piece with raised waist > 0399 > In the example here a whole hip piece is draped. **>>** First drape half a hip piece and mirror the other half. **>>** Pin CF to CF of the stand above the waistline. **>>** Pin a waist dart following the contour of the body upwards. **>>** Use tape to indicate the top of the hip piece. **>>** Mark the following lines: raised waist, darts and side seam. **>>** Remove the whole hip piece from the stand and true all the lines. **>>** Mirror the panel. Cut out the whole piece with seam allowance. **>>** Pin the hip piece together flat and check it on the stand. **>>** Fold the seam above the raised waist inwards.

0400

0401

Skirt piece > 0400 > Pin CF and HH line to the corresponding lines of the stand. **>>** Affix the side seam from HH line downwards. **>>** Cut in the toile up to 20 cm under the raised waist. **> 0401 >** Drape a half front panel; fold the point towards the opposite side and form the pleats in the band. **>>** If the band has too much fabric you can remove some from the side. **>>** Do the same with the other half.

0402

0403

0404

> **0402 / 0403 / 0404 >** Twist the two bands around each other and attach them at the side seam. **>>** Drape a back panel according to your own design. A half back panel is sufficient.
>> The side seam can be pinned straight, tapering or flared. **>>** Mark the following lines: side seam and the band where it is attached to the side seam.
>> Remove the whole piece from the stand and true all the lines. **>>** Cut out the panels with seam allowance.
>> Pin the panels together flat and check the model on the stand.

Charles Frederick Worth 1892

> **0405 / 0406** > Build up the correct volume by using a petticoat and a piece of fiberfill on the dress stand.

> **0407** > Prepare the toile for the first back panel. Place the CB line 22 cm from the selvedge. **>>** Pin CB onto the stand. Cut out the neckline and make nicks in the seam allowance.

> **0408** > Lay a pleat ± 5 cm deep to CB.

0407

0408

0409

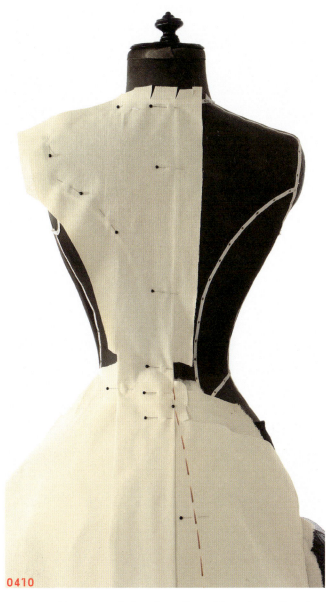

0410

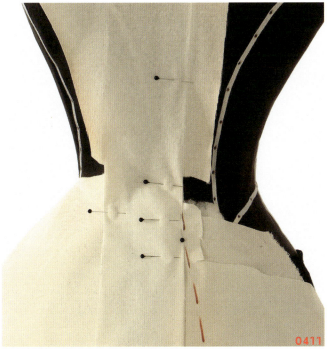

0411

> 0409 > Pin a second pleat 8 cm from CB so that a flat pleat is created from CB. >> Cut into the panel at waist height as far as CB and fold the pleat away from the bodice.

> 0410 / 0411 > Cut into the panel from the side seam to the pleat and fold the pleat away from the bodice. Smoothly pin the back panel of the bodice and pin the toile along the figure line and the arm hole. >> Cut along the figure line of the upper panel with seam allowance from waist height to the arm hole.

> 0412 / 0413 / 0414 > Pin the second back panel with straight grain onto the stand. **>>** Pin the seam and cut away surplus fabric at the arm hole.

0412

0413

0414

0415

0416

0417

> 0415 > Pin a third panel (a triangle) with straight grain between panel 1 and panel 2 ± 25 cm under the waistline. This is to create more space at the back of the skirt.

> 0416 / 0417 > Pin the bodice CF to the stand, cut out the neckline and make nicks in the seam allowance. **>>** Pin the toile along the figure line and cut away surplus fabric.
>> Pin the waist dart to just past the bust point and cut away surplus fabric.

0418

0419

0420

> **0418 / 0419** > Pin a fifth panel with straight grain onto the stand at the front and side. >> Pin the segment seam and the side seam in the front panel. > **0420** > Smooth the side panel towards CF and pin it to the figure line. > **0421 / 0422 / 0423** > Pin the sixth panel (skirt) CF onto the stand. This front panel hangs separately over the side panel almost as far as the side seam. >> Pin the waist-figure line from CF to the side seam. >> Decide on the length of the skirt.

0421

0422

0423

> **0424 / 0425 / 0426** > Make a one-piece straight sleeve (see p. 92). Pin the arm onto the dress stand. >> Take an ample piece of toile and pin it to the sleeve, upside down and puckered, just above the elbow. >> Lift up the toile, determine the volume and shape the sleeve head. Set it in fairly high and puckered.

0424

0425

0426

0427

0428

> **0427 / 0428** > Take a piece of toile cut on the bias and drape a collar on a somewhat deepened neck. The closure of the collar connects to the shoulder seam. >> Mark all the lines. >> Remove the whole piece from the stand and true all the lines. >> Cut out the panels with seam allowance. >> The example shows the panels mirrored. >> Pin the panels together flat and check the model on the stand.

0429

0431

0430

> *Christoff von*
> *Drecoll*

Christoff von Drecoll 1923

> *Christoff von Drecoll*

>> This asymmetrical model is draped on all sides. >> We use a thin, supple toile for a straight fall of the skirt. **Skirt** > Prepare a piece of bias-cut toile for the flared skirt (see p. 49). >> If the fabric is too narrow, a piece in the same grain can be attached to obtain the correct fabric width.

Front panel > 0432 / 0433 > Pin the toile to the middle of the stand next to the neck. >> Cut the toile at CF and form the flares from the waist by turning the toile downwards in the direction of the side seam. >> For each flare nick the seam allowance above the waistline.

> 0434 / 0435 > Do the same with the other half. >> Repeat the foregoing on the back.

Pin a tape around the waist so you can mark it off. >> Decide on the length of the skirt. >> Mark the following lines: waistline, side seams, CF and CB. >> Pin the side seams together flat.

0437

0436

Bodice > Front panel > 0438 / 0439 > First length > Prepare a piece of toile for the right-hand front from side seam to side seam. >> Pin CF and BW to the corresponding lines of the stand. >> Pin the right-hand waist dart diagonally towards the right-hand side seam. >> Pin the left-hand waist dart corresponding with the figure of the stand. >> Partly cut away the diagonal neckline.

0439

0438

0440

0441

> **0440 / 0441** > Mark the figure line of the front panel with tape.
Back panel > 0442 / 0443 > Prepare a piece of toile for the left-hand back panel
from side seam to side seam. >> Pin BW and CB to the corresponding lines of the
stand. Pin the waist darts in the panel parallel to the figure of the stand. >> Pin
the side seams. >> Mark the figure line of the back panel with tape, connecting it
to the front panel.

0442

0443

Second length > 0444 / 0445 / 0446 > Front panel > Prepare a piece of toile for the left-hand front from side seam to past the CF. **>>** Pin CF and BW to the corresponding lines of the stand. **>>** Pin the diagonal dart from the left side seam to the end of the panel. This dart is needed so you can form the curve of the waist in the panel. **>>** Use tape to mark the figure. **>>** Cut away surplus toile.

0446

0444

0445

0447

0448

0449

Back panel > 0447 / 0448 / 0449 > Prepare a piece of toile for the right-hand back from side seam to past the CB. **>>** Pin CB and BW to the corresponding lines of the stand. **>>** Pin the diagonal dart from the right side seam to the end of the panel. Pin the right-hand side seam. **>>** Use tape to mark the figure. **>>** Cut away surplus toile.

Third length > 0450 / 0451 > Front panel > Prepare a piece of toile for the left-hand front from side seam to side seam. **>>** Pin CF and BW to the corresponding lines of the stand. **>>** Pin the diagonal dart from the left bust point to the right-hand side seam as far as the end of the panel. **>>** Use tape to mark the arm hole and the figure. **>>** Cut away surplus toile.

0452

Back panel > 0452 / 0453 > Prepare a piece of toile for the right-hand back from side seam to side seam. **>>** Pin CB and CB to the corresponding lines of the stand. **>>** Pin the diagonal dart from the right side seam to the left side seam. **>>** Use tape to mark the arm hole and the figure. **>>** Cut away surplus toile.

0450

0451

0454

0455

> 0454 / 0455 > Mark all the lines and provide control points where the panels cross so the model can be accurately reassembled later. **>>** Remove the panels from the stand and true all the lines. **>>** If required, mark any extra width on the side seam. **>>** Cut out the pattern parts with seam allowance. **>>** Pin the panels together flat and check the model on the stand.

0453

0456

0457

0458

> *Madeleine Vionnet*

Madeleine Vionnet 1932

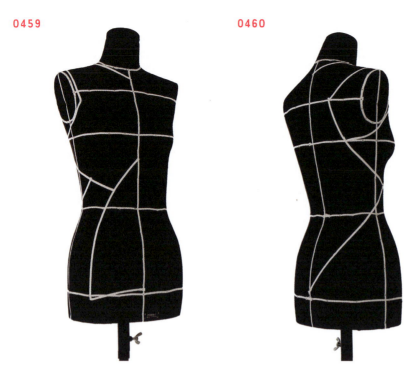

> **0459 / 0460** > Place figure lines on the stand before you start draping. > **0461 / 0462** > Prepare the toile for the first panel and indicate the straight grain on the fabric. >> Pin the toile on the bias to CF. >> Cut out the panel with seam allowance.

0463

0464

0465

0466

0467

> **0463 / 0464 >** Pin the second panel on the bias to CF on the stand. **>>** Cut out the panel with seam allowance. **>>** Pin the seams of panel 1 and 2 together across the previously placed figure line.

> **0465 / 0466 / 0467>** Prepare the toile for the back panel and indicate the straight grain on the fabric. **>>** Pin the toile on the bias to CB. **>>** Cut out the panel with seam allowance. Pin the shoulder seam and the diagonal side seam together. **>>** Make several nicks in the seam allowance to reduce tension on the seam allowances. **>>** Now you can see why the seam is placed here - there is so much tension on the fabric up to this point that it cannot be made flat otherwise.

> **0468** >Pin the bust dart parallel to the figure line of the back panel.
>> Mark all the lines in the middle of the bands on the stand.
> **0469 / 0470** > Prepare the toile for the flared skirt on the front and indicate the straight grain on the fabric.
>> Here the model is based on a whole front panel. The draped panel is later mirrored on the other half. You can of course also drape a half front panel.
>> Pin the toile on the bias at CB.
>> Cut the toile at CF to just above the join line of panel 2. >> Cut into the seam allowance where the flare is to be and turn the fabric down towards the side seam.

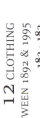

0471

> **0471 >** Pin the seam allowance of the skirt and panel 2 together.

> **0472 >** Pin a piece of toile cut on the bias to panel 1 and 2. **>>** Turn the toile downwards along the figure line of the back panel.

0472

> 0473 / 0474 > Make nicks in the seam allowance so the toile can be laid in a flowing line over the hip.
>> Continue working in this way to CB and let the skirt flare a bit more at the back. **>>** Pin the segment seam together.

0473

0474

0475

> 0475 > Pin the long skirt seam from panel 2 to the hem. **>>** Mark everything. Remove the panels from the stand and true all the lines. **>>** Pin the panels together flat and check the model on the stand.

0476

0478

0477

> *Madame Grès*

Madame Grès 1938

For this model a dress stand from the Fifties and early Sixties has been used since it better suits the model to be draped. >> The model in question here is asymmetrical and so the dress is draped in its entirety.

>> A stretch fabric is used so we can easily see how well the finished model falls.

> 0480 / 0481 > Prepare a large piece of fabric for the skirt. Indicate the lengthwise and crosswise grain in the middle of the piece (CB). >> Pin CB to CB of the stand. >> Cut out the waist-line with seam allowance and make nicks so that the waist can be laid nice and flat.

0479

0480

0481

0482

0483

> **0482 / 0483** > Fold the fabric forward and pin pleats in the left-hand part, turning the fabric upwards.
>> The pleats are placed left of centre. Fold the right side forwards and drape in the pleats. >> Pin the long skirt seam together. >> Cut away surplus fabric at the front. >> Mark waistline, pleats and seam. Indicate the pleats clearly so they can be properly reassembled later on.

0484

0485

> **0484 / 0485** > Pin an arm onto the dress stand. >> Prepare a large piece of fabric for the front panel and the sleeves. >> Mark CF in the middle of the piece. >> Pin CF to CF of the stand. >> Drape the pleats on the right-hand side of the bodice. At the waist they should run into the pleats of the skirt. You will need to stretch the stretch fabric a little for this.

> 0486 > Drape the pleats on the left-hand side of the bodice. These too are laid towards the waist. **>>** Cut vertically into the fabric on the left side. **>>** Cut horizontally under the waist line towards the pinned pleats of the bodice.
> 0487 / 0488 > Make a horizontal cut at CF for the neckline and affix it.
>> Fold back the remaining fabric for the back side and sleeve. **>>** Pin the bodice on the left side through to the back and cut out the arm hole.

0487

0488

0489

> **0489** > Make a vertical cut on the right side next to the pleats down to under the waistline. Cut out the waistline with seam allowance and make nicks in the seam allowance.
>> Pin the panel through to CB.
> **0490 / 0491** > The two upper panels are laid at the back. >> Pin CB together, make a number of pleats on either side of CB. >> Cut out the waist with seam allowance.

0490

0491

0492

> **0492** > Bring the fabric to the front. >> Pin in the sleeve seam in line with the neckline.

> **0493 / 0494 / 0495** > Pin the under sleeve seam through to the back and pin a back sleeve seam if there is not enough fabric left over to drape the sleeve in one piece. >> Mark all the lines and pleats. Remove the panels from the stand and true the lines. >> Mirror the sleeve for the other side. >> Pin the panels together flat and check the model on the stand.

0493

0494

0495

0496

0497

0498

> Christian Dior

Christian Dior 1950

0501

0499

0500

0502

Skirt > 0499 > The skirt consists of four panels with extra seams in the front and back panels. **>>** If you drape a half toile and mark CF and CB 4 cm from the edge of the fabric. For an entire toile you need a wider piece of fabric so you can later mirror the half skirt. **>>** The heavier quality of toile used for this model is similar to the sturdy wool used for the Dior jacket. **>>** Prepare the toile for the skirt. Indicate CF and HH lines.

Front panel > Pin CF and HH to the corresponding lines of the dress stand. Cut out the waistline and make nicks in the seam allowance. **>>** Use tape to indicate the figure line of the extra seam on the front panel. Mark the figure line. **>>** Cut out the front panel with seam allowance.

Side panel > 0500 / 0501 > Prepare the toile for the side panel. Place a grain line in the middle of the toile and mark the HH line. **>>** Pin the grain line in a straight line onto the stand. **>>** Pin together the extra seam, incorporating part of the waist dart. The space left over is later incorporated in a dart on the side. **>>** Cut out the extra seam with seam allowance.

Back panel > 0502 > Prepare the toile for the back panel. **>>** Mark the CB and HH line on the toile. **>>** Pin CB and HH to the corresponding lines of the stand. **>>** Cut into the waistline and make nicks in the seam allowance. **>>** Use tape to indicate the figure line of the extra seam on the back panel. Mark the figure line. **>>** Cut out the back panel with seam allowance. **>>** Pin together the extra seam, incorporating part of the waist dart.

0503

> **0503 / 0504** > Pin the remaining space in the side panel into a dart at the side seam. >> Mark the following lines: waistline, extra seams and dart. >> Decide on the length of the skirt. >> Remove the panels from the stand and true all the lines. >> If you are making a whole model the panels are mirrored for the other side.

0504

> **0505** > Pin the panels together flat and check the model on the stand. >> A tape has been pinned at the waist to make it easy to see when draping the top.

0505

0506

0507

0508

0509

Jacket > Panel 1 > 0506 / 0507 > Prepare the toile for the front panel. Mark CF and BW on the toile. **>>** Cut a piece off at the neck. **>>** Cut out the waistline and make nicks in the seam allowance. **>>** Use tape to indicate the figure line of the extra seam. The extra seams in this top have a distinctly fluid form. **>>** Mark the figure line (extra seam). **>>** Cut out the extra seam with seam allowance.

Panel 2 > 0508 / 0509 > Prepare the toile for the second front panel with a BW line and a grain line in the middle of the toile. **>>** Pin the panel with straight grain to the stand and pin the extra seam together. Cut away surplus fabric. **>>** Cut out the waistline and make nicks in the seam allowance. **>>** Cut out a small arm hole.

0510

0511

Panel 3 and panel 4 > 0510 / 0511
> Prepare the toile for the back panel with CB and BW lines. **>>** Use tape to indicate the figure of the extra seam, allowing it to connect with the extra seam of the front panel. **>>** Mark the figure line. **>>** Cut out the extra seam with seam allowance. **>>** Prepare the toile for the second back panel with a BW line and a grain line in the middle of the toile. **>>** Pin the panel with straight grain to the stand, pin the extra seam together and cut away surplus fabric. **>>** Cut out the waistline and make nicks in the seam allowance. **>>** Cut away a piece at the arm hole. Pin the side seam, which lies a little to the front. **>>** Pin the shoulder seam and cut out the side seam and shoulder with seam allowance.

> 0512 / 0513 > Cut away a piece at the arm hole at the back. **>>** Use tape to indicate the arm hole. Like the figure lines, this arm hole also has a specific form. The sleeve is set in fairly high. **>>** Mark the arm hole.

0512

0513

Tunic > 0514 / 0515 / 0516 > Pin a piece of fiberfill in the waist as extra support during draping. **>>** On all the following panels a horizontal and a vertical grain line is indicated. **>>** Pin a piece of toile in the waist under panel 2, cut out the waistline and make nicks in the seam allowance. **>>** Do the same in the waist under panel 3 and pin the side seam together.

0514

0515

0516

0517

0518

> 0517 / 0518 > Pin a piece of toile to CF. This panel runs from CF to the side seam. **>>** Cut out the curved line with seam allowance. This line connects up with the extra seam of the top. **>>** Pin a loose piece of toile cut on the bias behind the curved line of the pocket. Fold the curved line inwards so the figure line is easier to see.

> **0519** > Use tape to indicate the figure of the jacket at the bottom.
>> Mark this line.

0519

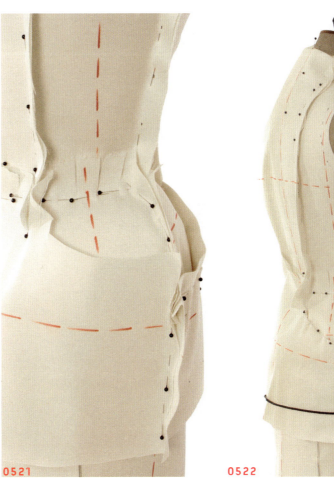

0520   **0521**   **0522**

> **0520 / 0521 / 0522** > Pin the back panel running from CB to side seam. >> As in the front panel create the curve towards the side seam by cutting away fabric and folding inwards. >> Use tape to indicate the figure of the jacket at the bottom. Mark this line.

> **0523 / 0524 / 0525** > Prepare a two-piece sleeve (see p. 96) with a little extra width. **>>** Pin the sleeve into the arm hole from FSC to BSC. Cut into the seam allowance at these points and fold the seam allowance outwards. **>>** Pin the head flat onto the stand at the marked-off arm hole. Excess fabric is incorporated in a dart in line with the shoulder seam. **>>** Mark all the lines. **>>** Remove the panels from the stand and true the lines. **>>** For a whole model the panels are now mirrored. **>>** Pin the panels together flat and check the model on the stand.

0523

0524

0525

0526

0527

0528

> *Christian Dior*

Christian Dior 1952

Bodice > Prepare the toile, indicating CF and CB lines. **> 0529 >** Place a petticoat (and in this case a layer of fiberfill as well) on the dress stand to get the right volume and silhouette. **>>** Hang the arm onto the stand in a slightly raised position (with a piece of toile or fiberfill under the armpit, for example).
> 0530 / 0531 > Pin CF and BW to the corresponding lines of the stand. **>>** Cut out the neckline fairly high and curved and make nicks in the seam allowance.

0529

0530

>> Pin the toile next to the bust and smoothly down along the side seam.
>> Space is created under the bust point. >> Cut away surplus fabric under the waistline and make nicks in the seam allowance so the waist can be laid smoothly. >> Starting at the waistline, pin the dart, which splits into two small darts just below the bust point.
>> Attach the toile to the shoulder and upper arm, making sure that you have enough fabric in the armpit for the under sleeve seam.
>> Cut out the shoulder and sleeve with seam allowance.

0532

0533

0534

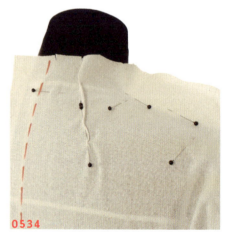

> 0532 / 0533 / 0534 > Pin CB and BW to the corresponding lines of the stand. **>>** Cut out the neckline high and make nicks in the seam allowance. **>>** Pin the shoulder dart towards the neckline so the neck can be laid smoothly.

> 0535 / 0536 / 0537 > Pin the shoulder and upper arm seams. >> Space is created in the waist; pin the waist dart together. >> Cut away surplus fabric under the waistline and make nicks in the seam allowance so the waist can be laid smoothly. >> Cut out the shoulder and upper arm seams with seam allowance. >> Starting at the waist, pin the side seams of the front and back panels together until there is so much tension that you can't pin any further.

0535

0536

0537

0538

0539

0540

> 0538 / 0539 > Cut the side seam with seam allowance and cut diagonally towards the uppermost pin. >> Pin the under sleeve seam from the wrist and make a dart at elbow height if necessary. >> Continue pinning the under sleeve seam to approximately the same height as the side seam. > 0540 > Make an incision in the front and back panels in the direction of the FSC and BSC. A gusset-shaped opening is created.

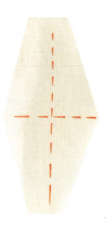

0541

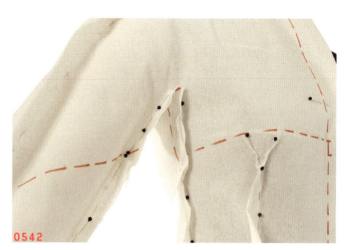

0542

0543

> 0541 / 0542 / 0543 > Pin the gusset-shaped gusset longitudinally from panel to sleeve.

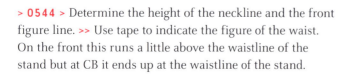

0544

> 0544 > Determine the height of the neckline and the front figure line. >> Use tape to indicate the figure of the waist. On the front this runs a little above the waistline of the stand but at CB it ends up at the waistline of the stand.

0545

Skirt > Prepare the toile for the skirt, indicating the CF and HH lines.
> 0545 > Cut a diagonal sloping point for the first panel and pin CF to the stand.

0546

> **0546** > Pin the second panel at the waistline and make nicks in the seam allowance so you can lay it smoothly in the waist. **>>** The skirt part will stick out at the hip because of the underlying fiberfill. **>>** Pin a seam for the figure line swelling somewhat across the hip.

0547

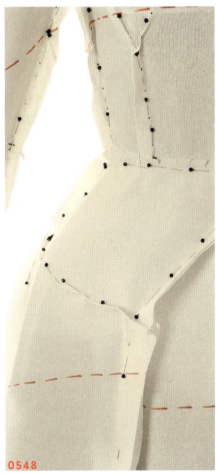

0548

0549

> **0547 / 0548** > Pin the seam of the first and second panel together. > **0549** > Pin a hip piece onto the stand at CB and use tape to indicate the figure line, which should connect up with the seam of the front panel. A flared skirt is pinned onto this figure line.

> 0550 / 0551 / 0552 > Pin the skirt part to the hip piece with enough fabric above the figure line and make flares in it. **>>** Cut into the toile horizontally from CB above the figure line, with seam allowance. **>>** Make nicks where the first flare appears. **>>** Turn the toile downwards to the side seam so you can form the flare. **>>** Pin the side seam running a little to the back. **>>** Mark all the lines. **>>** Remove the whole piece from the stand and true all the lines. Mark extra width if necessary. **>>** Cut out the panels with seam allowance. **>>** In the example shown the panels are mirrored. **>>** Pin the panels together flat and check the model on the stand. **>>** Decide on the length of the skirt.

0551

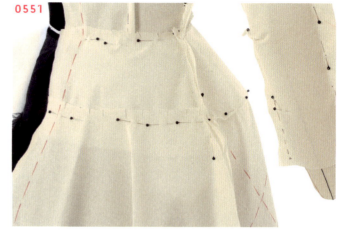

0550

0552

> *Christian Dior*

0553

0554

0555

> André Courrèges

André Courrèges 1965

> For this double-breasted A-line dress a heavier toile is used so that the silhouette comes across well. >> Prepare the toile for the shoulder yoke. >> Cut extra fabric at CF for the wide overlap. Indicate CF on the toile.

Front panel > 0556 > Pin CF to the stand and cut away a small part of the neckline. >> Pin a piece of black tape onto the yoke to indicate the figure line. >> Mark the figure line and cut out the yoke with seam allowance.

> 0557 > Prepare the toile for the front panel with a CF and a BW line. >> Pin CF and BW to the corresponding lines of the stand. >> Do not pin the toile to the waist since the dress is going to be flared. >> Pin the seams of the yoke and the front panel together. >> Use tape to indicate the figure of the vertical seam. >> Mark the seam and cut out the panel with seam allowance.

> 0558 / 0559 > Prepare the toile for the side panel of the seam extending to the side seam. Mark a vertical grain line and the BW line. >> Pin the panel with straight grain to the stand. Do not attach to the waist. Pin the vertical seam and the remaining seam of the yoke. >> Cut away surplus fabric. >> Cut out the arm hole.

> André Courrèges

0556

0557

0558

0559

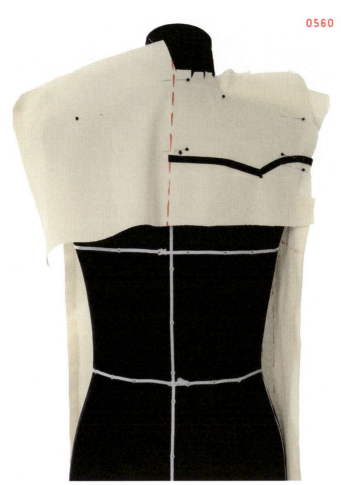

Back panel > 0560 / 0561 / 0562 >
Prepare the toile for the yoke of the back panel with a CB line. >> If you are draping half a toile, mark 4 cm at CB. >> Pin CB to the stand and cut out the neckline. >> Pin tape to indicate the figure on the yoke. >> Mark the yoke and cut it out with seam allowance. >> Prepare the toile for the back panel with a CB and BW line. >> Pin CB and BW to the corresponding lines of the stand. >> Pin the seam of the yoke and the back panel together. >> Place a piece of tape to indicate the figure of the vertical seam. >> Mark the seam and cut the panel out with seam allowance.

> **0563 / 0564** > Prepare the toile for the side panel, from the seam to the side seam. Indicate a vertical grain line and the BW line. >> Pin the panel with straight grain to the stand. Do not attach to the waist. >> Pin the vertical seam and the remaining seam of the yoke. >> Cut away surplus fabric.
>> Cut out the arm hole. >> Pin the side seam together following the form. The narrowest point of the dress is situated just above the waistline.
>> Mark the arm hole.

0563

0564

Sleeve > 0565 / 0566 > Prepare the toile for a one-piece sleeve with a little extra width (see p. 92). >> Pin the under sleeve into the arm hole from FSC to BSC, making a nick at these points. >> Pin the sleeve into the arm hole and cut away surplus fabric.

0565

0566

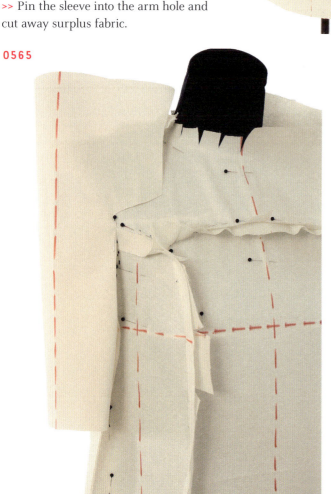

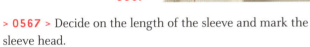

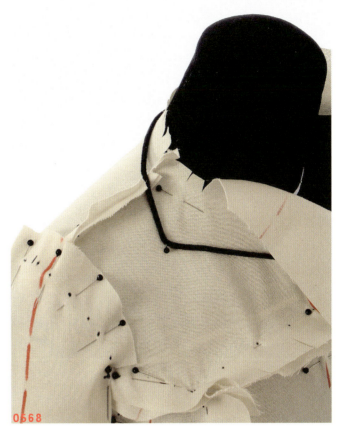

0569

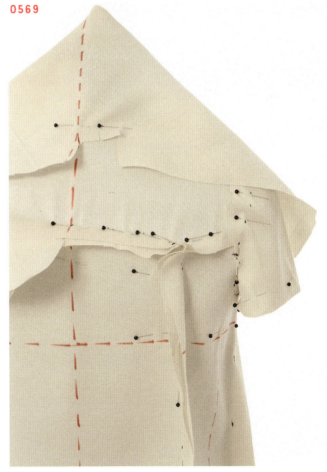

> **0567** > Decide on the length of the sleeve and mark the sleeve head.

Collar > **0568 / 0569** > Indicate the neckline with a piece of tape. Mark the neckline. >> Prepare a piece of toile cut on the bias for the collar. Place a CB on the collar part. Pin the collar part somewhat low so enough height is retained for laying the collar in a circle.

> 0570 / 0571 > Turn the collar forwards and attach it as far as the corner point in the front panel, making enough nicks towards the neckline. **>>** Fold over the collar and pin it in the form desired. **>>** Pin the lapel in the form desired.

0571

0570

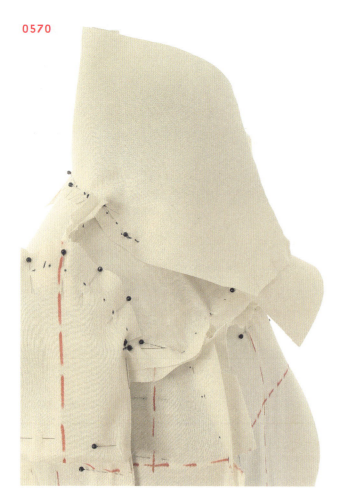

> 0572 > Pin a piece of tape to indicate the position of the pocket strip. **>>** Mark all the lines. **>>** Remove the panels from the stand and true all the lines. **>>** With a whole model the panels are mirrored for the other side. **>>** Pin the panels together flat and check the model on the stand. **>>** Place the buttons on the panel.

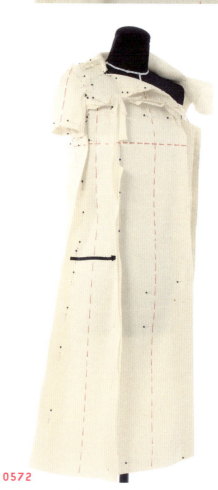

0572

0573

0574

0575

> *Yves Saint Laurent*

Yves Saint Laurent 1975

0576

0577

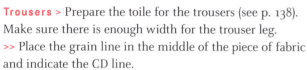

0578

Trousers > Prepare the toile for the trousers (see p. 138).
Make sure there is enough width for the trouser leg.
>> Place the grain line in the middle of the piece of fabric
and indicate the CD line.
> 0576 / 0577 / 0578 > Pin if needed a small pleat on the
grain line in the toile. **>>** Pin the grain line to the balance
line on the front of the leg. **>>** Pin the CD line to the corresponding line of the stand. **>>** Attach CF and cut away
surplus fabric above the CD line. **>>** Cut in the crutch seam
and shape it around the leg to the inner leg seam. Make
sufficient nicks. **>>** Pin the outer leg seam down in a straight
line. **>>** Pin the remaining fabric in the waist into a dart or
flat as a pleat.

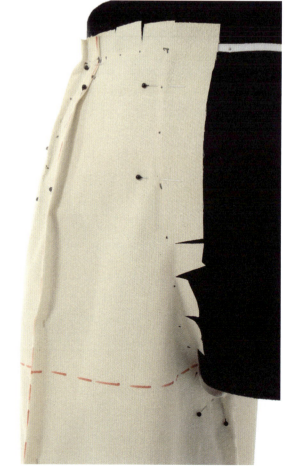

0579

0580

0581

> **0579 / 0580 / 0581 >** Prepare the toile for the back leg with the CD line and a grain line in the middle of the toile. **>>** Pin a small pleat on the grain line, making it disappear as it nears the waist. **>>** Pin the grain line to the balance line at the back of the leg. **>>** Pin CB and cut away surplus fabric along CB. **>>** Shape the crutch seam and pin the inner leg seam of the front and back panels together. **>>** Pin the side seam together. Cut away surplus fabric. **>>** Depending on the amount of space remaining in the waist, make one or two darts.

> 0582 > Pin a piece of tape to determine the position of the pocket. **>>** Mark all the lines, darts and pleat. **>>** Remove the panels from the stand and true all the lines. **>>** With a whole model the panels are mirrored for the other half.

> 0583 > Pin the panels together flat and check the model on the stand.

0583

0582

0584

0585

Jacket > Prepare the toile for the front panel. Place CF and BW lines on the toile. **>>** Allow extra width for the overlap. **>>** Pin a shoulder pad to the stand.

> 0584 / 0585 > Pin CF and BW to the corresponding lines of the stand. **>>** Cut out the neckline and make nicks in the seam allowance. **>>** Cut out the arm hole with ample seam allowance for the time being. **>>** Pin tape to the front panel to indicate the figure of the vertical seam. **>>** Mark the seam and cut away surplus fabric. **>>** Pin the seam onto the stand and pin a waist dart.

0586

0587

> **0586 / 0587** > Prepare the toile for the back panel with CB and BW lines. >> Place CB and BW onto the corresponding lines of the stand. >> The panel twists a little from the back at CB across the middle, for extra width at the seam. >> Cut out the neckline and make nicks in the seam allowance. >> Pin the shoulder seam.
>> Pin a tape onto the back panel to indicate the figure of the vertical seam. >> Mark the seam and cut away surplus fabric. >> Pin the seam onto the stand and pin a waist dart. >> Cut out the arm hole with ample seam allowance.

> **0588 / 0589** > Prepare the toile for the side panel with a BW line and a vertical grain line. >> Pin the grain line straight onto the stand. >> Pin the seams of the front and back panels against each other. >> Make sure the jacket has enough room at the bottom.

0588

0589

0590

0591

0592

Sleeve > 0590 / 0591 / 0592 > Use tape to indicate the arm hole and mark it. **>>** Make a two-piece sleeve (see p. 96). Hang the sleeve in the correct position in the arm hole from FSC to BSC. Nick into the seam allowance at these points and fold the seam allowance outwards. **>>** Pin the head of the sleeve into the arm hole and cut away surplus fabric.

0593

0594

Collar and lapel > 0593 / 0594 > Determine the width of the overlap and indicate the position of the top button. Cut in horizontally as far as the end of the overlap and fold over the lapel. **>>** Indicate the neckline. **>>** Prepare a piece of toile cut on the bias for the collar. **>>** Pin the collar onto the panel from CB.
>> Continue pinning the collar until a few centimetres past the shoulder seam and attach the collar to the lapel.

> **0595 / 0596** > Fold down the collar and lapel and lay them flat on the panel, making sure there are no kinks in the foldline. >> Use a piece of tape to indicate the shape of the lapel.
>> Indicate the figure line of the lapel on the collar. >> Pin the lapel and the collar in the form desired.
> **0597** > Decide on the length of the jacket. Mark all the lines. Remove the panels from the stand and true all the lines. >> With a whole model the panels are mirrored for the other half.
>> Pin the panels together flat and check the model on the stand.

0595

0596

0597

0598

0599

> Pierre Cardin

Pierre Cardin 1979

Skirt > 0600 / 0601 / 0602 > Prepare the toile. Take a piece of fabric from CF to CB with extra width at CF and CB. **>>** Place a vertical grain line in the middle of the toile and the HH line.

0600

0601

0602

0603

> 0603 > Pin the straight grain line and the HH line to the side of the stand. **>>** Turn the HH line, CF and CB upwards a little so extra space is created in the waist and the skirt tapers towards the hem. **>>** Pin the pleats in front and back panels. Cut out the waistline with seam allowance.

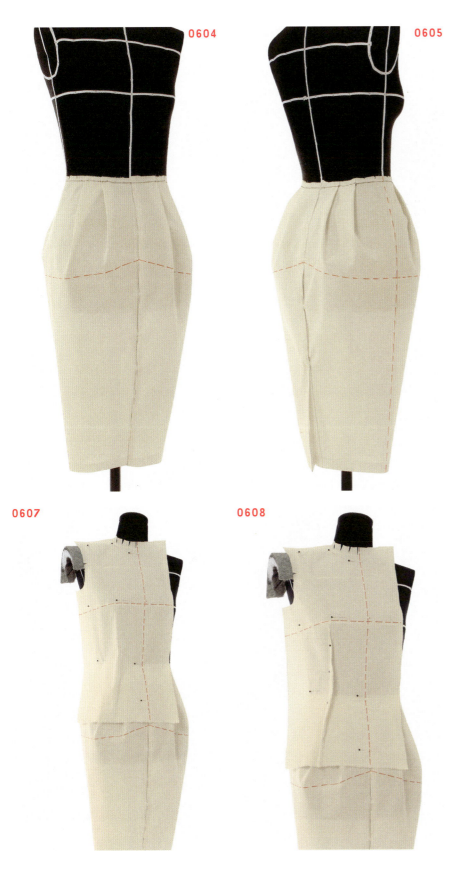

0604

0605

0607

0608

0606

> **0604 / 0605** > Mark CF and CB.
>> Mark the pleats. Remove the panel from the stand and true all the lines.
>> With a whole model the panel is mirrored for the other side. >> Pin the panels together flat and check the model on the stand. >> A split is incorporated in the CB seam.

> **0606** > First place a high shoulder pad onto the stand so that the shoulder line runs horizontally. >> Pin a piece of tape across the shoulder pad to indicate the arm hole.

> **0607 / 0608** > Prepare a front panel as far as the side seam with a CF and BW line. >> Cut extra fabric at CF for the overlap. >> Pin CF and BW to the corresponding lines of the stand.
>> Cut out the neckline and make nicks in the seam allowance. >> Cut out the arm hole with seam allowance. >> Pin the side seam. >> Pin the waist dart. Make some space at the hem.

0609

0610

> **0609 / 0610** > Prepare the back panel with a CB and BW line. >> Pin CB and BW to the corresponding lines of the stand. >> Cut out the neckline and make nicks in the seam allowance. >> Cut out the arm hole with seam allowance. >> Pin the waist dart. >> Pin the side seam together. Make some space at the hem. Cut away surplus fabric. >> Decide on the length of the jacket. >> Since the shoulder is so horizontal the shoulder dart is probably not needed.

0611

0612

0613

> **0611 / 0612 / 0613** > Pin the shoulder seam flat. >> Prepare a large piece of fabric with a vertical grain line in the middle. >> Draw two horizontal lines on the toile - one at elbow height and one on the upper arm. >> Pin the straight grain line to the inside of the arm, mark the arm hole and cut it out with seam allowance. >> Fold the toile around the arm and attach it to the panel at FSC and BSC. Make nicks at these points so that the toile lies smoothly across.

0614

0615

> **0614 / 0615 >** Prepare a long, narrow strip with a length from the neckline to the wrist. **>>** Indicate the vertical grain in the middle of the strip. **>>** Indicate the elbow line and the upper arm. **>>** Unpin the shoulder seam and pin the strip to the front panel and along the sleeve.

0614

0615

> **0614 / 0615 >** The strip should be at a right angle to the end of the shoulder pad. **>>** Pin the back panel and the sleeve to the inserted piece in the same way as to the front panel. **>>** Decide on the length of the sleeve.

> **0616 / 0617 / 0618 >** Use a piece of tape to indicate the neckline and mark it off. **>>** Take a piece of toile cut on the bias and pin CB to CB of the neckline. **>>** Turn the toile up and forwards and pin the collar onto the neckline.

0616

0617

0618

0619

0620

0621

> **0619 / 0620 / 0621 >** Fold and cut the collar in style. **>>** Mark all the lines, remove the panels from the stand and true all the lines. **>>** With a whole model the panels are mirrored for the other side. **>>** Pin the panels together flat and check the model on the stand.

0622

0623

0624

> *Yohji Yamamoto*

Yohji Yamamoto 1995

> This design consists of different materials and is therefore draped in different materials: a stretch fabric for the bodice and robust cotton for the skirt. > **0625** > Pin two arms onto the dress stand in the position shown in the illustration so the bodice can be draped. > **0626** > Prepare the stretch fabric for the front panel, indicating CF in the middle of the piece. >> Pin CF to CF of the stand. >> Pin the stretch fabric smoothly across the bust to the side. >> Cut into the fabric under the waistline to prevent pull. >> Use black tape to indicate the figure of the front panel (seam). >> The seam runs beside the bust point.

0625

0626

0627

0628

> **0627 / 0628** > Prepare the stretch fabric for the back panel. >> Place CB to CB of the stand. >> Use black tape to indicate the figure of the back panel (seam). >> Cut into the fabric under the waistline. >> Prepare a piece of fabric with a vertical grain line for the side panel. >> Pin this piece to the front and back panels. >> Cut into the fabric under the waistline.

0629   0630

0631

> **0629 / 0630** > Prepare a long piece of stretch fabric to run from the seam in the back panel, across the arm and along the front to CB + extra length. >> Place a vertical grain line on the fabric. >> Pin the grain line to the grain line of the arm. >> Attach the fabric to the opposite side seam.
>> Pin the fabric to the seam of the back panel. >> Cut away surplus fabric at the back.
> **0631** > Pin the fabric to the seam of the front panel.
>> Cut away part of the fabric above the bust and pin the shoulder cap. >> Pin the sleeve to the desired length and cut away surplus fabric.

0632

0633

> **0632 / 0633** > Use black tape to indicate the neck line in the front and back panel. > **0634 / 0635** > With a whole model the panels are mirrored for the other side. >> Pin the panels together flat and check the model on the stand.

0634

0635

0636

0637

> **0636 / 0637** > Prepare the toile for the skirt. This piece is 1.75 cm long and 80 cm wide. **>>** Indicate CF and HH lines on the toile. **>>** Pin CF 3.5 cm past CF in the waist, and HH line to the HH line of the stand. **>>** From this new waist point turn the fabric down at a slant so that a diagonal over-lap is created. **>>** Turn the piece of fabric through to CB.

> **0638 / 0639 >** At CB the HH line corresponds horizontally with the HH line of the stand. **>>** Above the waistline cut into the fabric parallel to the waist and a little further than half the side panel. **>>** The space created in the waist is taken up with small pleats in the front and back panel. **>>** The long strip remaining above the waist is folded loosely across the arm to CB and attached.

0638

0639

> **0640 / 0641 >** Mark CB on the strip. **>>** Mark the new CF, pleats, waist and CB of the skirt. **>>** Remove the panel from the stand and true all the lines. **>>** With a whole model the panels are mirrored for the other side. **>>** Pin the panels together flat and check the model on the stand.

0640

0641

0642

0643

0644

Glossary

AHC
Arm hole circumference

AL
Arm length

Balance line
This line runs vertically in the centre of the front and back leg from waist to foot

BD
Bust depth

BL
Back length

BSC
Back sleeve cross mark

BW
Bust

BAW
Back width

CB
Centre back

CD
Crutch depth

CF
Centre front

Construction lines
Lines drawn onto the toile with a red ballpoint or fineliner

Cutting clean
Cutting off the seam allowance

Draping
Draping fabric to make a garment

Dress stand
Dressmaker's dummy for working on

EW
Elbow width

Extra width
Extra space marked off after draping

FCW
Front chest width

Fibrefill
Synthetic filling

Figure lines
Lines applied to the stand or the model with white or black tape

FL
Front length

Flare
By turning the fabric extra space is created in a panel

FSC
Front sleeve cross mark

FW
Foot width

Gored
Extra width

HH
Hip height

HW
Hip

KH
Knee height

KW
Knee width

LAL
Lower arm length

LL
Leg length

Marking
During or after draping a black ballpoint pen or fineliner is used to indicate the pinned lines, seams or figure lines on the toile

Mousseline
Toile used for draping in earlier times

NW
Neck width

Permanent demarcation lines
Lines attached to the stand corresponding to the lines on the toile

Pinning flat
The one seam allowance is folded over and pinned onto the other seam so the model can be put together

Preparing the toile
Pulling straight, ironing and applying lines

Seam allowance
Extra fabric on a panel so that the design can be pinned together

SL
Side length (also known as outside leg length)

SW
Shoulder width

Tape
Narrow twilled tape used for indicating figure lines on the stand or toile

Toile
Fabric used for working with, or the final model

Toiliste
Person who makes toiles

UAW
Upper arm width

ULW
Upper leg width

WC
Wrist circumference

WW
Waist

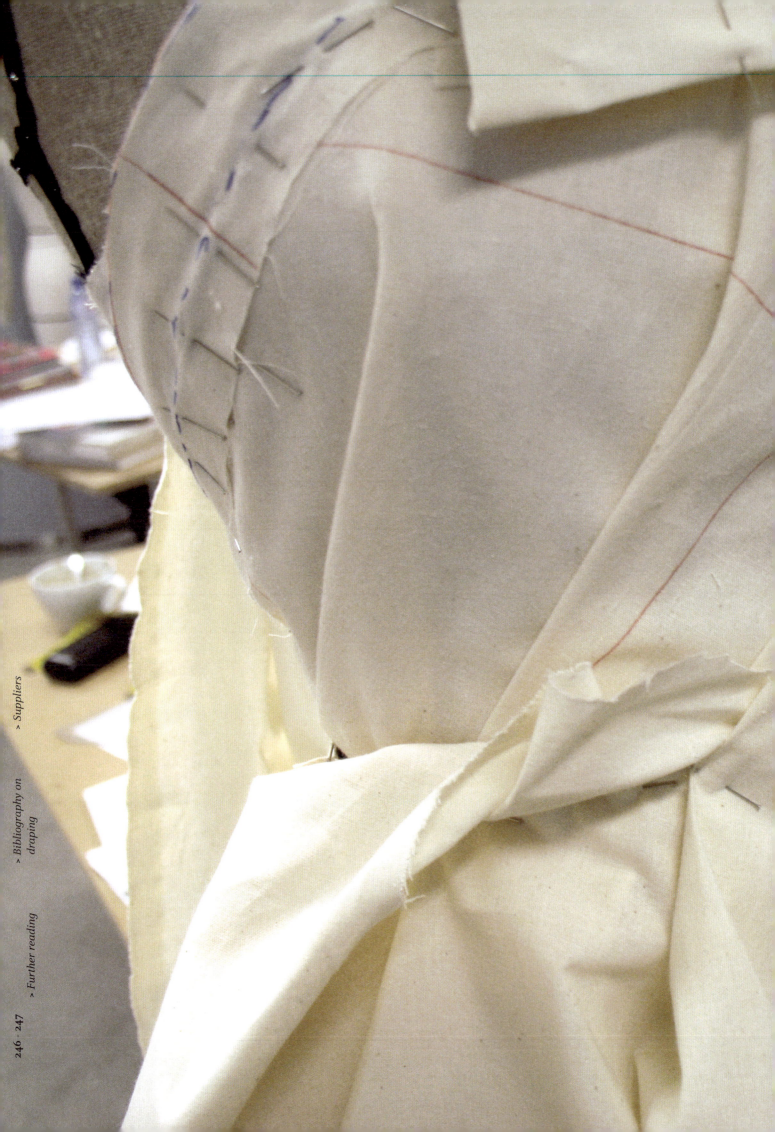

Further reading

Bibliography

Suppliers

Books on sewing

The present book is limited to an extensive study of the art of draping and deliberately does not deal with sewing techniques, about which there are several good books available. We would particularly recommend:

Couture Sewing Techniques
Claire B. Schaeffer
ISBN-10: 0942391888
ISBN-13: 978-09423918886

Tailoring
The classic guide to sewing the perfect jacket
Creative Publishing International
ISBN-1: 58923-230-5

Books on pattern making

All sorts of materials dealing with two-dimensional pattern making are available, including the German Rundschau System or Cad/Cam pattern design software. Various methods have also been published in book form.

Bibliography on draping

Mme Berge, *Coupe et Assemblage par le Moulage*, Vuibert et Nony Éditeurs, Paris 1907

Annemarie Bönsch, *Formengeschichte europäischer Kleidung*, Böhlau Verlag GmbH, Vienna/Cologne/Weimar 2001

Pamela Golbin (ed.), *Balenciaga Paris*, Thames & Hudson Ltd., London 2006

Lydia Kamitsis et al., *Madeleine Vionnet, Keizerin van de mode*, Gemeentemuseum Den Haag, Waanders BV, Zwolle 1999

James Laver, *Costume and Fashion. A Concise History*, Thames & Hudson Ltd., London 1985

Janice Mee, Michael Purdy, *Modelling on the Dress Stand*, BSP Professional Books, Oxford 1987

Catalogue Modemuseum Antwerpen, *Patronen, Patterns*, Ludion, Antwerp 2003

Caroline Rennolds Milbank, *Couture*, Stewart, Tabori & Chang, New York 1985

Eduard van Rijn, *Mouleren en Draperen*, Cantecleer, De Bilt 1989

Suppliers

Dress stands
As far as the correct dress stand is concerned it is important that it meets the requirements of use (see p.30 - 31).
For professional use a stand has to meet the necessary measurements and proportions.
Stockman supplies various types of figures.
Primafit stands are very easy to work with.

Siegel and Stockman
www.siegel-stockman.com

Colophon

5th Edition, 2017

Authors

Annette Duburg, Rixt van der Tol

Author of 'History' and 'Contemporary Designers': Karin Schacknat

Editors

Jan Brand, Minke Vos

Translation Dutch-English

Michael Gibbs

Photography

Hans Vroege

Peter Stigter: p. 20 and p. 24

Technical drawings

Rolf Beelen

Design

ArtEZ University of the Arts,

Cindy van der Meijden and Margot Wolters,

With thanks to Rein Houkes and Thomas Castro

Production

Colour & Books, Apeldoorn

Printing

Wilco Art Books, Amersfoort

With thanks to

Jos Beek, Marco Bolderheij, Martin van Dusseldorp, Fashion Institute Arnhem, Willem Hillenius, Leslie Holden, Michiel Keuper, Eduard van Rijn, Els Roseboom, Tim van Steenbergen, Ger Strijker, Jeroen Wande- maker, department of fashion design ArtEZ University of the Arts; with special thanks to Matthijs Boelee, Jeannette de Saint Obin and Wendy Barten

Distribution

Idea Books

Nieuwe Herengracht 11

1011 RK Amsterdam

The Netherlands

www.ideabooks.nl

ArtEZ Press

Jan Brand, Minke Vos

P.O. Box 49

6800 AA Arnhem

The Netherlands

www.artez.nl/artezpress

ArtEZ Press is part of ArtEZ University of the Arts

ArtEZ Press

ISBN 978-94-91444-21-0

NUR 452

This book is also available in Dutch: ISBN 978-90-89100-86-3